Wrestling Old Man Market

Wrestling Old Man Market

Real world insight and best practices to institutional investing told through the experiences and wit of a former college wrestler and fund manager.

Trip Rodgers, CFA

Library of Congress Control Number: 2015920660

ISBN:	Hardcover	978-1-5144-3506-9
	Softcover	978-1-5144-3505-2
	eBook	978-1-5144-3504-5

Print information available on the last page.

Originally published: 02/12/2016
Rev. date: 09/24/2016

To order additional copies of this book, contact:
Xlibris
1-888-795-4274
www.Xlibris.com
Orders@Xlibris.com
731359

Table of Contents

To my three awesome kids.

Introduction

It's 5:45am and my alarm clock is going off with its usual unpleasant awakening. Normally, my response would be a reflexive slap in the direction of the snooze button. But not today. Because this morning I've already been up waiting on the clock for the last 15 minutes, just like I was up tossing and turning at 2am, 3am, and 4:30am. I hate that, but insomnia is inevitable on nights like this. For today is probably the biggest day of the year for my portfolio and certainly one that could be a turning point for me at the hedge fund where I work. My largest position in my portfolio reports earnings today. Sure, that happens four times a year. But today's announcement is particularly critical, as it follows a disappointment last quarter and management's assurance to the Street that it was a one-off occurrence and did not signify any issues at the company. Today, the company either shows it is back on track or that it's on a distinct downhill trajectory. If it's the latter, the market will not likely be kind. In fact, the importance of the earnings number to be released and management's guidance (probably equally important) has already been well recognized, as the stock's implied volatility in the options market has suggested a large move in either direction. I anxiously check my email on my phone immediately from bed, but no press release yet. I know that it isn't due for another hour or two, but I figured I would check anyway.

Like most portfolio managers at a hedge fund, the vast majority of my compensation comes in the form of a bonus that is directly tied to my P&L for the year. Equally as important in this business, if you find yourself on the losing end too often, returns deep into the red can mean game over before you even get to the end of the year. So my stress is not unfounded, nor is it uncommon. Still, I have to focus on one day at a time. And today, I need to be on my game. I have conviction in my position. I've done the work. I've followed this stock for years. I know the company inside and out. I've visited their facilities. I've met with management. I've talked to all the sell-side analysts covering the company. I've chatted endlessly with several of my peers at other firms who also know the stock. I've talked to traders, industry contacts, and competitors. I've modeled the financials and gone over various earnings scenarios and sensitivities. I've examined short interest levels and know the bear case. I'm in touch with sentiment. I've mapped out at what levels and under what scenarios I would add to the position and why I would unwind it. I've done the work. I am prepared.

Still, as I drive to work, I feel the butterflies in my stomach. I grin for a second as I think about one of my favorite expressions in the business. "Today, will I be the bug or the windshield?" It seems very applicable this morning. But reflecting on the humor doesn't relax me much. I'm too focused today.

As I drive in, I turn off the radio and start to mentally get my head in the game and reflect on all my work. Quickly though, my thoughts start to drift. The butterflies seem very similar to another time in my life. My thoughts take me back over twenty years to when I was a Division I collegiate wrestler. Yes, wrestling. Not the kind where there are ring ropes, a guy in a mask, and an obnoxious announcer. I'm talking about the real kind of wrestling with real wins and real losses that starts in the pee-wee division and, as you grow, defines who you are and who you will be. It's the kind of wrestling that can take you as far as you want, even the Olympics, if you have the proper dedication, the drive, and the attitude to push on through the enviable setbacks and injuries. There are no short cuts to get there.

Today's churning in my stomach is just like the feeling I would get in the moments before a big match. I remember it vividly. I recall my warm-up ritual, the drills that were instinctive for so much of my life, the pre-match stretching and visualization. I remember looking across the mat at my opponent, who is also warming up and going through his own pre-match ritual. Like often the case at this level, he's a formidable adversary. I hear he was a state champion in high school. But so was I, and so was almost everyone who has made it this far. And I think he's ranked nationally. But

I've beaten higher-ranked wrestlers. Such rankings are arbitrary anyway. They don't mean anything. I try to avoid these mind games, but sometimes they slip into your thoughts.

Once in high school when I was wrestling in Germany on a summer Jr. USA team, I saw my opponent smoke a cigarette before our match. That was pretty amusing. However, I don't think this guy is about to light up. Like me, he recognizes the importance of this match to both himself and to his team.

As I put on my headphones, I see him look over my way. I wonder if he has the same thoughts. Is he thinking about my strengths or my toughness? Does he appreciate all my victories? Does he know the sacrifices I've made to get here? The countless hours of hard work, all the years of training and big matches, the hundreds of practices since elementary school that have prepared me for moments such as this. Does he understand my willingness to lay it all on the line for seven minutes and leave nothing on the mat? He probably does. He's likely made the same sacrifices, endured the same pain, dropped the same amount of weight, and drilled the same number of hours. He and I are of the same cut. The same mentality. The same toughness. But does he want it as much as me? That we'll find out very shortly.

I snap out of my trance thankfully before I hit a double-leg on the receptionist as I walk into the office. Back to the present day where my opponents are at other funds and wear suits and button-downs, not singlets. Still, the atmosphere here can be just as intense. Confidence is paramount in this game, just as it was when I was about to walk onto the mat. I respect my opponent, but I believe in myself even more. I've worked too hard for this. I deserve to be successful.

At my desk now, I see S&P futures are higher. It looks like it's going to be a good day for the market. But will it be a good one for my book? It's largely unrelated, particularly on big event days like today. As I wait for the press release, the butterflies are back and I feel a little more tension in my body. The familiarity of competition returns. I thrive on moments like this. It's all on my shoulders. Time to show what I'm made of...how good I really am.

I ignore a few less-pressing phone calls and let them go to voicemail. The market will open shortly after the release and quickly reflect investors' response on the company's share price. Then, I will have to decide my move. Will I sell, buy more, or sit on the sidelines and just observe the chaos? I check my screen for news and quickly review my model, almost like some last minute pre-match stretching. It's now getting close to the release time. I close my eyes and picture myself walking onto the mat and shaking my opponent's hand. The release is out. The referee blows the whistle. It's go time.

****

"So what's your point of writing all this?" as I'm sure my closer friends will ask. "Doesn't the world have enough investment books and articles or whatever this is?"

Fair questions. And probably a "yes" to the second one. Maybe let me start with describing what this is by highlighting what it is not:

1) **It's not any ivory tower investment mumbo jumbo.**

I have great respect for the work of authors of all those articles in professional journals on various investment topics, many of which actually seem interesting when reading the summaries upfront. However, where they lose me (and most readers I think) is when they feel compelled to complicate each topic with purely academic jargon or some long formula, which somehow describes their work, yet only reminds me of a calculus exam I bombed in college. I understand that the math is often necessary and serves as a validation of their work, but it doesn't exactly make for good reading or something that seems very applicable to most people with investment jobs in the real world.

So, I'm going to take a different tact. I'm going to strive to make this as little theoretical and academic as possible. I'm not going to reveal some new investment theory or challenge the academic work of others. I understand some people are intrigued by that sort of stuff. But again, while I respect the work, the day-to-day applicability of much of it seems rather negligible to me. Rather, what I'm going to share here are just my thoughts and stories based on my real world experiences from roughly 20 years on both the buy- and sell-side. Some of it may be fairly obvious material to many in the investment business. But I'm going to try not to complicate it and just leave it at that.

[Quick break for basic definition clarification: The sell-side is essentially all broker-dealers involved in the selling of securities (e.g., stocks, bonds, derivatives). They include the large bulge bracket banks, mid-size brokerage firms, and boutique research/sales/trading shops. They make money through trade commissions from either (or both) institutional and retail clients, as well as in most cases through investment banking fees from corporate clients. The primary sell-side positions that will be discussed here are research analysts/associates, who publish reports and offer their opinions about publicly-traded companies; institutional salespeople, who market the research to clients; and traders, who execute the buying and selling of the securities. The buy-side are the institutional clients of the sell-side. They are the money managers. The buy-side is broadly separated into two groups. The first is long-only managers, who only take ownership positions in securities, such as mutual funds and pension plans. The other group consist of hedge funds and the like, who are able to both own securities and sell-short securities, as well as engage in other creative investment strategies.]

2) **It's not an attempt to even the score or get anything off my chest.**

My parents have always taught me that life is too short to hold grudges. And fortunately, I've had little reason to. I've have had good working relationships with nearly all my colleagues during my career, and I have developed a number of good friends through work for which I'm extremely blessed. Sure, there are a few people I could have done without and a few where I've had to reexamine my opinion over time. However, holding on to bitterness truly serves no purpose. There are a lot of difficult people in the world, and many of them unfortunately seem to find their way to the investment industry. But, I've found taking a positive tact with those types is generally the easiest and best way to go. Moreover, any past confrontations or ill will toward those people has to be viewed as water under the bridge. Stewing over such things is just wasted time and hampers you in productively working towards what's next.

3) **It's not to complain about the increasingly difficult environment in the securities business.**

In just about all areas of the investment industry, business seems tougher today than it was in past decades. Technology, increased competition, new investment products, and heightened regulations have had the general effect of making it more difficult to earn a buck, or more accurately millions of bucks, than was the case in the past. Crowdedness in the hedge fund arena has been well documented for several years. Nevertheless, it remains an important issue today, causing stocks' daily moves to be more volatile and unpredictable than in decades past. Also, high frequency trading and algorithm programs have complicated the trading aspect of the business. As a consequence, it is no surprise that in recent years some well-known, experienced hedge fund owners have thrown in the towel and closed their funds.

Elsewhere, the long-only side of the business has greater competition from passively-managed funds, such as today's more readily-available electronically-traded funds (ETFs), which generally come with lower fees to investors. Finally, on the sell-side, the vast number of brokerage firms, combined with price decimalization and rules that have further separated capital markets and investment banking, have made that part of the business less lucrative and more challenging as well.

I could go on and on and sulk why our beloved securities industry has been ruined. But, we all must deal with the environment we are currently in and make the best out of it. Moreover, none of the factors that have made the business more difficult nullify what are still the best approaches to making money and the most effective ways to conduct yourself with regard to the market. One of my favorite investing books is "*Reminiscences of a Stock Operator*" by Edwin Lefevre, originally published in 1923. While the book is nearly a century old and relates to public markets where the rules were very different than current times, its key points are still incredibly insightful and relevant today. The playing field may have changed, but the core fundamental principles to investing and how to approach capital markets remain consistent with those of past decades.[1]

4) **It's not about assigning blame or credit.**

I hate name-dropping, possibly because, according to my wife, I'm not very good at remembering names in the first place. So for my writings here, I've intentionally left out the names for the most part, not to protect the innocent, but just because that seemed easiest and I didn't want to upset anyone either by including them or by leaving them out.

5) **It's not directed to only those in the hedge fund business.**

Admittedly, much of my investing thoughts and opinions have been formed from my hedge fund experiences. Nevertheless, I believe most of what will be discussed is also relevant to long-only investing and securities analysis in general.

Still, let me make one point of clarification up front. I tend to use the terms "an investment" and "a trade" interchangeably. I know some people see them in very different lights. The long-only crowd rolls their eyes at the mentioning of a stock being only a trade, as if all hedge fund managers are Texas gunslingers sitting on trading floors just impulsively shuffling stocks around.

Similarly, the hedge fund community rolls its collective eyes on the thought of being stuck with a stock because it's an investment that you must hold on to come hell or high water since "you're in it for the long-term." Maybe everyone can just agree to disagree here and accept whichever terminology I use.

6) **It's not a victory lap.**

Like most Portfolio Managers (PMs), I've had some good years and some, let's call it, less-good years. The latter has definitely kept my ego in check and given me great respect for the market and the difficulty in consistently generating strong returns. That was especially the case when I was running a paired equities, market-neutral strategy (a portfolio strategy that seeks to eliminate systemic risk, or market risk, by buying one stock and selling short another stock by the same amount from its peer group and maintaining a portfolio of pairs that sum to near zero net market volatility, or beta).

7) **It's not a review of my investment thoughts regarding current events or concerning certain companies or sectors.**

That's not my point here. There is more than enough of that stuff out there already. Plus, I believe a key issue today with most research is a lack of shelf-life. I hope that will not be the case with this missive.

8) **And it's not that long.**

A friend of mine who is a sell-side research analyst encouraged me to write this, but told me to keep it relatively short. "No one really has the attention span or desire to read too much of this kind of stuff."

After years of experiencing a barrage of emails, voicemails, and other time drains, I've gained a greater

> appreciation for the value of my time. As such, I get frustrated when someone shows little respect for it. For instance, it is apparent that some equity salespeople erroneously measure the quality of a call by how long they keep their client on the phone. Similarly, many sell-side analysts think the longer the report they write, the more likely it is to be read. Sure, I've always appreciated insightful sales calls and in-depth analysis from analysts. But in most cases, as a PM, what I really needed was the quickest and most efficient means to attain the information so that I could move on to the countless other things I needed to read and address. Typically, that wasn't a 3MB-sized report in my inbox. Even if they seemed interesting, I often moved those emails to a file called "read later," to which I almost never did. So again, with all that in mind, I'll try to make this less like "*War and Peace*" and more like something you could finish on a long plane ride (assuming you skip the movie).

In short, the agenda here is to explore what I believe are some of the key tenets in institutional investing, in particular dispelling the idea of a secret sauce, as well as walking through some core thoughts on contrarian investing. I'll offer a number of recurring factors that often present the opportunity to capitalize on a change in a stock price, as well as detail the process one might follow when researching an idea. In the later chapters, I will emphasize the necessity for maintaining a well-crafted thesis for a position and examine other important investing topics, including timing, confidence, common sense, savviness, and coping with the day-to-day stresses of the business.

Many of the discussions in this book may be best suited for those already employed in the investment business or those seeking a career in the sector. Still, I hope it is also worthwhile for more casual investors, particularly in gaining an appreciation for the competitive investing field and the processes and qualities needed for success in analyzing securities or managing a portfolio.

With all the challenges in the market and large number of participants, it's easy to grow a bit cynical on certain aspects of the investment management business and the stock market in general. Still, I strongly believe being a successful PM, analyst, or everyday investor is not arbitrary. There is a definite set of traits and learned expertise that makes a person successful in this business, just like with any industry. My objective is to share some of the knowledge, strategies, and best practices I've learned over the years and that I've been fortunate to witness among very talented colleagues. That encompasses a lot of learning and a lot of experiences, much of which I probably will not even recollect for this. Nevertheless, when it comes to focusing on the core broad factors to be successful in the investment management business, I go back again to my wrestling years and the three keys I believe it takes to be successful there:

i) **Have great technique (or skills).** In wrestling, you need to know the moves and be proficient in when and how to use them. Similarly, in investing, you must have the financial, deduction, research, and problem solving skills to excel in the job. It's no secret that without learning and applying those, it's hard to compete.

ii) **Repetition**. In wrestling, as with any sport, once you know the moves, you have to practice them over and over until they become second nature. The end result is that you become confident and effective in any position or circumstance presented to you. In investing, it's called experience. You learn by doing and you learn from your mistakes. By being exposed to various situations and events, you gain perspective and confidence that greatly benefits you the next time those situations and events come around. Randy Pausch in *The Last Lecture* said, "Experience is what you get when you didn't get what you wanted. And experience is often the most valuable thing you have to offer."[2] I certainly feel that has been true in both my athletic and professional career.

iii) **Be tough.** You can't get around this one in wrestling. You need both the mental and physical toughness to outlast your opponent and not succumb to the desire to quit when things get difficult. This has pertinence with many jobs, but particularly in the securities business, where you must possess the toughness to withstand the constant attacks on your knowledge base, conviction levels, and specific ideas. Most importantly, when the market inevitably knocks you down, you can't wallow in self-pity and sulk why things are not going your way. You have to get up and fight on. Each day is a new day and an opportunity to get back on the right path.

"Allow me to lend a machete to your intellectual thicket."

Captain Jack Sparrow, Movie: Pirates of the Caribbean

Chapter 1:

The Secret Sauce

One of my memories as a kid growing up in rural Oklahoma was of my mother's creative cooking. Not that she was a bad cook. In fact, as a growing boy, I always remembered rather liking the food at our dinner table. Nevertheless, our mother was probably a bit more "resourceful" than the average mom when it came to food. To quickly explain, our house was an inconvenient three country miles from the grocery store in the bustling metropolis of Blackwell (pop. 8,000 give or take). So understandably wanting to avoid the possibility of hitting rush hour traffic (generally meaning more than one vehicle on the road) or just the hassle of getting the car out of the garage, my mother often improvised around dinnertime when we were short of an ingredient or condiment in the cupboard. My most notable recollection of this concerned Thousand Island salad dressing, which my mom sought to convince my sisters and me was the real store-bought original. But, in actuality, her secret was no more than equal parts ketchup and mayonnaise with a little hot dog relish mixed in (if available). Delicious, right? Who could ever tell the difference?! So when we poured that delectable combination onto our lettuce, as well as onto basically any food that was fried (which included much of the menu), we credited mom for ingeniously and resourcefully coming up with her own "secret sauce" substitute for Thousand Island dressing.

Decades later my mother still enjoys cooking every so often, particularly for my folk's ten grandchildren. But now with the convenience of living closer to grocery stores and restaurants in Oklahoma City, the reliance of concocting such a secret sauce in her life is much diminished. Unfortunately, that's not the case for many participants in the investing world, who actively seek out and rely upon a secret sauce of investing by way of a set formula, style, or pattern in efforts to attain superior returns.

I've been in the securities business roughly two decades on both the buy- and sell-side. That's not quite long enough to recall the horrors of Black Monday. (I was busy dealing with the horrors of puberty then.) But, it's long enough to have learned a few things about investing and securities analysis. One of those being that the idea of a secret sauce in investing is a farce. Many have claimed success in the market through back-testing precise strategies or highlighting a strict investing regimen. However, whether evidenced by the market humbling the numerous debunked quant funds or socking it to stubborn investment managers unwilling to display any flexibility in their strategy, there are sufficient numbers of examples showing that there is no one successful fail-proof style or formula that can be trusted upon to consistently work year-in and year-out in our dynamic world of capital markets. (Sorry to those seeking an easy answer who eagerly paid $39.95 for a trading program sold on an infomercial or a larger amount for a one-day conference held at an airport hotel.) In fact, even the notion of a one-size-fits-all, "close your eyes and trust the program" solution or algorithm that can be successfully repeated is insulting to the thousands of highly-educated people employed in the global securities sector, whose work every day ensures the market to be a far more dynamic and complicated mechanism (or often more accurately described "opponent") than many give it credit for. So, again for the record, let me be very clear: THERE IS NO SECRET SAUCE!

Overconfidence and Randomness

What is it then that gives many investors a genuine state of overconfidence? What is the reason behind their steadfast belief that they will not succumb to the common driving emotional pitfalls of fear and greed, and that they are part of the very select crowd of active portfolio managers that are able to consistently outperform their benchmark?

In psychology, the condition is called "*Illusory Superiority*," or simply the tendency of individuals to overestimate their abilities relative to their peers. It's a common occurrence that exists far beyond the world of investing.[1,2] Be it in sports, politics, or even dating, overconfidence runs amuck in our society. Heck, it's probably the reason Las Vegas even exists, since most visitors honestly don't travel to the middle of the desert contemplating the possibility of having *less* cash in their pockets on their return flight. In their minds, too many people think, "That loser may have dropped all his money at the casino tables, but I'm too smart and too lucky for that to happen to me." It seems crazy that anyone could really think that illogically, yet it's sadly commonplace.

Perhaps overconfidence is simply a matter of being naive. Maybe inexperienced investors just *have* to fail at some point, or at many points, before they can recognize and give reverence to the complexity of financial markets. And, should they survive to play on, they are likely to be better ultimately for having learned the lesson. As I was told by an experienced PM when I joined the buy-side, "Investors and traders are like motorcyclists. There are those who have fallen and those that will."

Thus, during my years spent analyzing the pricing of stocks and the information influencing them and occurring numerous spills myself, I've increasingly gained respect for the market (or again "my opponent") and its frequent unwillingness to behave as I think it should, particular in the short term. Another seasoned buy-side friend once told me that he pictures the market as an old, distinguished wise man sitting in front of a fireplace, looking into your eyes as he swishes his glass of Cognac, anticipating your next mistake and rebuking your simplicity in thinking he should behave a certain way just because it is logical or has happened that way in the past.

That brings up the possibility of pure happenstance. Is it possible that events or performances in the market are not logically connected, but happen largely by chance and cannot be counted on reoccurring in any pattern or with any frequency? Does this Old Man Market really have no rhyme or reason to his ways?

I enjoyed reading the book "*Fooled by Randomness*" by Nassim Nicholas Taleb, also the author of "*The Black Swan*." "*Fooled by Randomness*" is an intriguing and intellectual book, which makes some excellent points. The narrative is fairly complex at times. Nevertheless, I think the major takeaway of the book is really in the title itself. Things are often more random than we realize or want to believe.[3]

We are so often fooled by thinking each event in life has to have a logical explanation or could have been foreseen if we had just better studied the fundamentals, patterns, or tendencies of the particular subject matter. We want to have reasons why things didn't go as we planned. But, in actuality, many things are just random. And that applies to investing, particularly in the short term. Sure, you can correlate the market's performance to some measurable factor in vogue like dividend yield or price momentum. But, it has been well broadcasted that people have also successfully (and ridiculously) correlated the market's performance to extremely arbitrary occurrences, such as the winner of the NFL's Super Bowl being from the NFC or the AFC division.

As shown in the following table, the annual return of the S&P 500 index has been positive 85% in the years when a team from the NFC conference won the Super Bowl, with an average return of 11.2%. That compares to a much lesser 65%, with an average return of 4.9%, in the years when the AFC won.[4,5] Of course, that's very nice and interesting, unless you decided to play the "Super Bowl Theory" in 2008 when the NFC's New York Giants stunned the undefeated New England Patriots, yet the financial crisis took the S&P 500 index down 38.5% for the year. And you would be similarly unhappy if you were bearish the market because the AFC won the big game in 2009 or 2013, years when the S&P 500 went on to jump 24.5% and 29.6%, respectively. Therefore, it seems the "Super Bowl Theory" is like most market correlation strategies which follow the common phrase "it works until it doesn't."

The reality is randomness is a possibility we just don't often want to consider, particularly when something positive occurs. In order to support our egos, it is common that we attribute our successes, and successful investments, to our self-perception of possessing above average skill or great intellect. Back to the concept of "Illusory Superiority." But, market participants should be honest with themselves and consider questions like, "Was it really my great intellect that got me to buy shares in a company that was shortly afterwards acquired by a competitor at a large premium, or was it just my turn to have a big winner?" Or, "Did that hot portfolio manager who was hired away to another fund only to have a terrible year suddenly lose his edge or his superior understanding?" Maybe his hot streak was random to begin with? This begs the question should funds confront the tendency of survivorship bias and engage in a strategy of seeking out the smart, but underperforming PMs who appear to be "due"?

Exhibit 1: Winners of Super Bowl Vs. Annual Return on S&P 500

Year	Winner	Conference	S&P Return	Year	Winner	Conference	S&P Return
1967	Green Bay	NFC	20.1%	1969	New York Jets	AFC	-11.4%
1968	Green Bay	NFC	7.7%	1970	Kansas City	AFC	0.1%
1972	Dallas	NFC	15.6%	1971	Baltimore	AFC	10.8%
1978	Dallas	NFC	1.7%	1973	Miami	AFC	-17.4%
1982	San Francisco	NFC	14.8%	1974	Miami	AFC	-29.7%
1983	Washington	NFC	17.3%	1975	Pittsburgh	AFC	31.6%
1985	San Francisco	NFC	26.3%	1976	Pittsburgh	AFC	19.2%
1986	Chicago	NFC	14.6%	1977	Oakland	AFC	-11.5%
1987	New York Giants	NFC	2.0%	1979	Pittsburgh	AFC	12.3%
1988	Washington	NFC	12.4%	1980	Pittsburgh	AFC	25.8%
1989	San Francisco	NFC	27.3%	1981	Oakland	AFC	-9.7%
1990	San Francisco	NFC	-6.6%	1984	Los Angeles	AFC	1.4%
1991	New York Giants	NFC	26.3%	1998	Denver	AFC	26.7%
1992	Washington	NFC	4.5%	1999	Denver	AFC	19.5%
1993	Dallas	NFC	7.1%	2001	Baltimore	AFC	-13.0%
1994	Dallas	NFC	-1.5%	2002	New England	AFC	-23.4%
1995	San Francisco	NFC	34.1%	2004	New England	AFC	9.0%
1996	Dallas	NFC	20.3%	2005	New England	AFC	3.0%
1997	Green Bay	NFC	31.0%	2006	Pittsburgh	AFC	13.6%
2000	St. Louis	NFC	-10.1%	2007	Indianapolis	AFC	3.5%
2003	Tampa Bay	NFC	26.4%	2009	Pittsburgh	AFC	24.5%
2008	New York Giants	NFC	-38.5%	2013	Baltimore	AFC	29.6%
2010	New Orleans	NFC	12.8%	2015	New England	AFC	-0.7%
2011	Green Bay	NFC	0.0%				
2012	New York Giants	NFC	13.4%			**average**	**4.9%**
2014	Seattle	NFC	11.4%			**# of up years**	**15**
						% of up years	**65.2%**
		average	**11.2%**				
		# of up years	**22**				
		% of up years	**84.6%**				

Conversely, when we do fail and are unsuccessful, we are more open to the idea of randomness and often chalk it up to "bad luck" and being at the wrong place at the wrong time. Naturally, we do this to protect our ego and prevent our confidence, or overconfidence, from being deflated. We've all heard the football quarterback who threw four interceptions talk after the game about tough conditions or great plays by the defense, rather than his poor decisions or bad passes. It's human nature not to blame ourselves. Investing is no different. Often portfolio managers do not come to the realization that only slightly more than half of their trades need to be profitable, perhaps a 60% completion percentage or so (sticking with the football analogy), to win the game. Instead, he or she is loath to admit their poor investments and tries to make them work at any cost rather than throwing the ball away. Later, we will discuss "hope trades" and allowing one bad investment to dominate the entire performance of a portfolio.

Therefore, with the need for appropriate market reverence and the potential for pure randomness in mind, I'm often amazed by the overbearing brashness of many analysts and PMs who place low probabilities on being wrong and in turn become vulnerable to the negative consequences of overconfidence. For one, they seem to have no appreciation that there are likely many handfuls of market participants just as smart and just as hard-working, who are analyzing the same information as they are. This was reinforced to me on several occasions at sell-side investor conferences in New York, Boston, Chicago, etc. While conversing with other attendees between management presentations or at dinners, I've often learned that a piece of information or my understanding of a company that I thought was so unique and proprietary was widespread knowledge among many of my peers. They were also highly driven, highly educated, and highly compensated, providing the same motivation that I had to dig in their heels to learn the details of a particular stock. Thus, the "edge," however great or small, I thought I possessed was in several cases actually part of the consensus thinking or was at least well-known by many people influencing the stock price on a daily basis. Of course, I'm not saying the information necessarily must have already been fully discounted in the stock price. In fact, holding the consensus view might have been a profitable choice. Still, a key lessen I learned is that it is critical to understand whether your ideas and opinions are well-known and part of the consensus, or if you truly have a contrarian or unique stance.

Wall Street compensation levels go in cycles and are typically quite volatile. Nevertheless, the investment business is still generally a very lucrative field, both on the buy- and sell-side. As a result, it tends to attract some of the smartest and most driven people in the world. So it's no surprise that competition is intense. Combined with the large number of firms on both sides of the business, this naturally makes the potential of attaining a truly unique or unmasked understanding of a company substantially more difficult, especially for the more widely-followed larger capitalization stocks (e.g., the Apples, GEs, and Amazons of our investing world).

Having a unique understanding is particularly arduous if your point of view was gleaned from the sell-side, where the primary jobs of salespeople and research analysts are to shout their thoughts from a megaphone in hopes of getting credit for the information in the form of client commissions or votes in popular investor surveys. In recent decades, the electronic age of emails and the internet has ensured that sell-side research is disseminated immediately and, in most cases, simultaneously. This has eliminated any timing advantage that was once prevalent in the business. Previously, research was distributed via mediums like the blast fax (as proof to my starting level on the totem pole, operating one was once one of my main responsibilities) or by sending hard copies by snail mail. That's probably inconceivable by young people entering the business today.

Similarly, regulatory filings by companies (e.g., 10Ks and 10Qs) that often included new, important information were also sent out by mail. Thus, being the first to receive one was a distinct advantage. In fact, for locally-based companies we followed on the sell-side, I remember rushing over to a given company's headquarters as soon as a major filing was available to be one of the first to receive a hard copy. Then, we would hurry back to the office to call our buy-side clients and read to them the key points from the filing. Amazingly, that was only two decades ago, although it seems like the dark ages now. In essence, the inefficiencies then without electronic dissemination resulted in an ability to provide information that was not immediately spread throughout the market as it is today. Therefore, it was much easier for some investors to obtain a competitive advantage.

A bit closer to modern day, in 2006, a group of employees from FTN Midwest left that firm to form a competing local institutional broker called Cleveland Research. The basis of the new firm was very logical: perform high-quality research and restrict the client base to 125 of the largest accounts in the U.S.[6] As a result, these top clients pay slightly more than the average going rate for the limited-access research, which largely comprises of market surveys on issues surrounding the companies they cover. Cleveland quickly became one of my favorite firms (and still is), as they employ some of the brightest analysts on the Street, and I believe their surveys provide extremely useful company and industry insight. Unsurprisingly though, I was not the only one to have this high opinion of their research product. Over time, the large number of the 125 firms that both receive and closely read their research became more than enough to influence opinions and stock prices in fairly short order after the research is published. Also, the firm's surveys have been broadly sought out and at times unavoidably have found their way to investors outside of Cleveland's client list. Therefore, Cleveland's research, while very insightful and worthwhile, may have become a bit less actionable to trading-oriented clients receiving it, as it often has rather quickly influenced the consensus thinking surrounding a stock. That was probably inevitable given the popularity of the firm and high quality of the work.

In October 2000, in an effort to level the capital markets playing field, the Securities and Exchange Commission (SEC) ratified and began to implement Regulation Fair Disclosure (Reg FD), which forbids companies to share material, nonpublic information in a private manner.[7] For both buy- and sell-side analysts, this naturally lessened the prior advantage of being in close contact with the management team of a company or even simply listening to company conference calls, which previously were not open to small investors in most cases. In the pre-Reg FD days, an analyst's relationship with a company was especially critical since management would often open up more to some analysts than others. Sell-side analysts who wrote research on the companies typically had the best access to management. This was frequently at the help of their investment bankers, who on the other side of the public information "wall" may have been assisting the company with corporate finance transactions. The closeness of those research analysts to management naturally increased the proprietary value of the research they published.

In fact, in the pre-Reg FD era, many companies tended to skirt the issue of giving formal earnings guidance, but rather "blessed" earnings models that were *faxed* to them from sell-side analysts. The level of feedback from management would vary from "your bottom line figure is too high" to "your revenue line should be closer to $xxxx." Of course, comments to the latter would eliminate much of the work related to the financial modeling process.

In one instance involving an industrials company we followed in the mid-1990s, my lead analyst and I were trying to get the CFO of a company to bless our earnings estimate for the next fiscal year of $2.25 per share. After asking several times, the CFO finally acquiesced and said, "Fine, that number looks good." He then called the CEO, who was on the golf course, and told him he had blessed the number. From my understanding, the CEO then responded, "What?!! We can't do $2.25!" The company the next week issued a press release estimating the next year's earnings near $1.50 per share, immediately sending the stock crashing down and the CFO out the door shortly after. That was just one example of many of how a lack of strategy and organization in communicating with the Street was big problem in the pre-Reg FD years. Although, it still is for many companies today.

Exhibit 2: Regulation Fair Disclosure

Regulation FD addresses the selective disclosure of information by publicly traded companies and other issuers. Regulation FD provides that when an issuer discloses material nonpublic information to certain individuals or entities—generally, securities market professionals, such as stock analysts, or holders of the issuer's securities who may well trade on the basis of the information—the issuer must make public disclosure of that information. In this way, Regulation FD aims to promote the full and fair disclosure.

Source: Fast Answers (www.sec.gov/answers)

Undoubtedly, Reg-FD cleaned up much of the informality and favoritism that was prevalent in companies' dealings with Wall Street and which was a key influence on stock prices for decades. Since then, most public companies are rightfully cautious to not step over the line by offering material information that has not been widely disseminated. This has made the work of analysts and investors more difficult, but perhaps more differentiated at times, as they must form their views through public information and the mosaic of nonmaterial details.

A Less Precise Recipe

Please note that even with the increased number of very capable market participants and new rules aimed at leveling the playing field, I am not making the case for an efficient market here or that Old Man Market with the glass of Cognac can't be beat. **My main point with all of this is that capital markets, or more precisely stock picking, should be approached with more thoughtfulness, respect, and a less precise investment recipe than many managers and investors often apply.**

Let me back-peddle a bit and admit that I believe factor-based investing can be successful at times. Such a strategy involves picking stocks that fit a certain criteria like a low Price/Forward EPS (PE) ratio, a high dividend yield, positive earnings revisions, or share price momentum. In particular, I strongly agree that screening for cheap stocks (those with the factor of having a relatively low earnings multiple, like PE), combined with attractive growth prospects, is a good place to start when searching for opportunities.

A friend of mine runs a small systematic fund or, in other words, a fund that is driven by a strict criteria across the portfolio rather than by selecting securities though bottoms-up research. He recently showed me a chart of the most successful investment factors over the past decade. At the top of the list was earnings multiples (i.e., buying cheap stocks), followed shortly by a couple momentum indicators. Near the bottom of the list of successful strategies was following sell-side analysts' recommendations. I particularly loved that, as it showed quantifiably what many of us in the business already knew. (As a former sell-side analyst, I'm allowed to say that.) Naturally then, doing the opposite of sell-side recommendations was near the top in terms of successful factors in selecting stocks. That follows what I've frequently said about my career, "On the sell-side, I needed to be smart, but not necessarily right, and on the buy-side I needed to be right, not necessarily smart."

The chart my friend showed me was undeniably interesting and gave the impression that one just needs to rigidly follow those factors at the top of the chart to derive a portfolio of outperforming stocks. And then you can go sit on the beach and watch your account grow. However, after talking to him for a while, it became apparent that his fund was more than just a "follow the formula and put it on auto-drive" strategy. His outperformance seemed also highly tied to manual tweaks, active monitoring of one-off events, and being aware of issues like sector concentration. Also, he's a pretty savvy guy with an MBA from a prestigious school and a plethora of contacts in the business, which helps. So again, I'm not dismissing his success. I'm just saying I don't believe generating strong returns is as simple as following the set factor performance chart he shared with me (his secret sauce). Logically, the strategy of following a particular factor for too long is doomed to fail, as other market participants also ultimately recognize and seek to exploit the success of that factor. The resulting overcrowding then generally ensures underperformance to other less-popular factors.

So what about something less complex? What about the rules-of-thumb in investing we have all heard so many times?...such as buying a stock after it splits or after it crosses a milestone figure like $100/share, or purchasing it two days after a big sell-off. After all, if such strategies hadn't had some success, they wouldn't be rules-of-thumb.

Early in my stint on the buy-side, I had a boss that gave considerable credence to such rules. One day, I was in an ornery mood and suggested to him that we employ a strategy of buying stocks with a three-letter ticker symbol and shorting stocks with a two-letter ticker symbol. Thus, with the arbitrage, we would "get a free call option on the third letter." I kept a serious face while he actually thought about it for a bit. He finally stormed away, muttering something about wondering why I was ever hired. Fortunately, I wasn't the only smartass in the group that suggested such things, so he quickly forgot about it. Also, it was after market hours, which is key if you're looking to pull jokes on bosses in the investment world.

That prank signifies what I think of such rules and their place in real investing. Although, I admit I have tried several times to apply the "two-day rule" as a portfolio manager (buying a stock two days after a major sell-off). In fact, we had a smart summer intern from the Booth School of Business at the University of Chicago once do a study on the two-day rule, to which he found no statistically significant proof of outperformance over any time period using the strategy of buying industrial and materials stocks two days after a big drop. So much for that idea. Again, I could picture Old Man Market in front of the fire shaking his head at my failed simplicity.

So what is there then? What is the key to sustained investment outperformance? Or, how does one generate significant profits that are unrelated to the overall market action, also called "alpha?" Finally, how does consistent outperformance occur when randomness seems often the driving force of the day or when one's playbook must be scrutinized and altered for each situation?

I have nothing against style bias. In fact, I would probably fit into the classification of a value investor based on my investing preferences and the industries I've historically followed. And I admit, rightfully or wrongly, I also often rely on "trusted" approaches, biases, and analysis that has worked successfully with prior investments. **Still, I believe the ideas of style or learned biases should be largely deemphasized with respect to what is the real key to investment outperformance. That is simply the diligent pursuit of identifying and correctly acting upon mispriced securities.**

OK, no kidding, right? Also, kind of broad and simplistic you're probably saying. However, if it was so easy, the possibility for security to be meaningfully "mispriced" obviously would not exist, as any potential excess return would be easily recognized and would be quickly arbitraged away. The fortunate issue for us non-indexers though is the inherent disagreement among market participants on which securities are mispriced and to what extent and direction. This makes the term "mispriced" quite subjective of course, as the classification is dependent on the numerous forecasting, valuation, and even behavioral elements of investing.

The extent of the mispricing inevitably depends on one's calculation of the "price arbitrage" opportunity being presented. Simplistically, "price arbitrage" is the difference between a security's current value and the estimate of its fair value. Unlike risk arbitrage strategies, where the discount to a stated acquisition price or ratio is readily known, the wide range of fair value estimates among market participants often leads to dramatically differing buy/sell/hold opinions of the security. It is this range of opinions and estimates of fair value which themselves influence the market price and create the belief among some investors that a security is mispriced. Nothing really too complicated there.

But then there is the issue of timing. After you have correctly identified what you believe is a mispriced security, how long must you wait until the security reflects a price closer to your estimate of fair value? This could be a short-term mispricing, perhaps for a beat-up stock that is the result of a potential overreaction concerning an issue that has little bearing on its longer-term future. In these cases, the overreaction is often quickly corrected as value buyers recognize the opportunity. Alternatively, for a company that has a track record of poor operational performance or has lost credibility with the Street, it may take several quarters or years for financial performance or sentiment to improve and for the company's long-term fair value to be better reflected in the market.

In either case, the efficient market hypothesis is discredited generally by the existence of an element of the story which is being incorrectly valued in the current price. That element may even be well-known. But once identified, the key then becomes a greater understanding of that element, the market's (i.e., your peers) knowledge of and sentiment toward the element, its probability of becoming greater in importance, and somehow quantifying the element via its potential effect on future revenues, earnings, value to the company, etc. More on all of this in the next chapter.

Additionally later, we will thoroughly discuss the process involved in the diligent pursuit of the mispricing or, in other words, our methodical uncovering and understanding of the element being mispriced. Of course, no successful means of stock picking is really superior to another as long as the end result is the same. Just as a golfer who hits a beautiful ball and spins it back to the hole receives the same score as the one who hits a "ground-burner" that somehow finds the bottom of the cup. Similarly, an investor can realize a large profit in a stock without ever understanding the true reason why they have done so or what the mispricing was attributed to in the first place. This generally adds to his or her overconfidence and blurs their reality that there is a scant chance of them continuing to do so with any consistency. Instead, just like the golfer with good form, **the ability to consistently select good investments requires the discipline to pursue a deeper understanding of the issues, a solid process, and the savvy to know when to put the trade on.**

The key word here is discipline. If there is a secret sauce out there, I believe that's it. There are multiple meanings for the word "discipline." To the negative, it's the corrective action we take with our children to show them right from wrong. And, to the positive, it is an unyielding, persistent mindset or course of action. As an ultimate example, Jesus Christ's closest followers who became the leaders of the early Christian church were called "disciples," illustrating their dedication and steadfast commitment to the new faith.

In wrestling, over the years, I've observed and studied many very successful competitors, both on a national and global level. They all had various strengths that were key to their victories. Some had great technique, some were immensely strong or had excellent endurance, some were tall with superior leverage, while others were more compact and explosive. Again, there was no magic formula. But, the one common denominator of all the successful wrestlers I've known is that they were all extremely disciplined. They took their competition and their preparations very seriously. They didn't cut corners or become complacent. They were focused and diligent in the pursuit of their goals.

Likewise, success in the securities business demands discipline of the same sort. The stigma frequently held by the general public of portfolio managers (particularly at hedge funds) seems to be of someone who makes buy/sell decisions largely on impulse. However, in reality, the opposite is true. Successful investors generally are those that are disciplined across the board, in their research, in their thought process, in their synthesis of the information, and in their process in general. If you're not willing to have discipline, you're likely to have a tough time when you tangle with Old Man Market.

"Ned, I would love to stay here and talk with you....but I'm not going to."

Phil Connors (played by Bill Murray), Movie: Groundhog Day

Chapter 2:

Resisting the Lure of the Free Taco

In 2011, our home team, the Dallas Mavericks, had a tremendous season and a marvelous playoff run to win the NBA championship, beating the formidable Miami Heat, led by LeBron James. Having never before won the championship, the Mavericks entered the playoffs with a 57-25 record and as the number two seed in the Western Division. This created quite a buzz in the DFW Metroplex, particularly as it followed another disappointing season by so-called America's team and my childhood favorite, the Dallas Cowboys. This buzz was best evidenced by the exciting atmosphere at home games, as Dirk Nowitzki, Jason Kidd, Jason Terry, et al typically delivered the crowd what they came for...another Mavs victory. Oh, that and a coupon for a free taco. ...Huh? OK, maybe that wasn't a significant prize for Mavs fans, but that's what one of the major Mexican fast food chains gave every attendee when the Mavericks finished a home game on top. As such, home victories were capped by the big screen blinking in bold letters, "MAVS WIN"....."FREE TACO."

This seemed like normal advertising to me and I never thought much about until Game 6 of the Western Conference Championship when the Mavericks hosted the Oklahoma City Thunder. Given the enormity of the game, I thought for sure when the Mavs won the hard-fought contest, the big screen would read "WESTERN CONFERENCE CHAMPIONS!" But instead, the same message from the regular season came up on the big screen and had my friends and me jumping up and down, yelling and laughing "FREE TACO!"

I tell this story because it's one my favorites and it allows me to recollect on that fabulous season, which unfortunately has yet to be repeated by the Mavs. It also is a good illustration of a focus on undoubtedly the wrong thing, as the big screen operator evidentially didn't recognize the significance of the win…or maybe the fast food chain simply paid up to advertise in the post-season as well. In any case, my point is the misguided focus on the free taco, rather than the Western Conference Championship, is similar to the market's frequent nature with many stocks to also focus in the wrong direction or to get hung-up on a trivial topic rather than what truly matters to the long-term viability of a company.

Of course, big moves in stock prices are often justified because of major announcements or results that differ meaningfully from the Street's expectations and require large recalibrations in the earnings outlooks for companies. In many instances, those announcements or results are ample reason to change one's calculation of a stock's intrinsic value. Still, there are many other cases that have analysts, traders, and investors scratching their heads that a piece of news which seems rather inconsequential in the long run could dramatically alter the market's valuation of a company. This is partially puzzling if that news has little effect on the longer-term cash flows of the corporation, since we know by financial definition that a company should be worth the present value sum of its future cash flows.

There are handfuls of examples of what appear to be overreactions each day in the market. But let me quickly discuss one that comes to mind. On July 29, 2014, a machinery company in my investment universe, Oshkosh Corporation (NYSE: OSK), fell 14% when it reported disappointing second quarter results.[1] I fortunately did not have a position in OSK at the time, but noticed the opportunity when the stock was crushed primarily because of a shortfall in its year-over-year incremental margin, the operating profit margin on sales that are in excess to sales in the same period a year ago.

$$\text{OSK's 2Q14 incremental margin} = \frac{(\text{Operating Profit } \mathit{2Q14} - \text{Operating Profit 2Q13})}{(\text{Sales 2Q14} - \text{Sales 2Q13})}$$

The large reaction seemed unjust to me, as management had explained the lower margins were mainly due to added new product development costs in the quarter and start-up costs at a new regional location, both of which would not be repeated. Why the big stock price decline then? What did investors expect? Did they think management should have ordered its new products group to cut spending late in the quarter or to push back the new location just so Oshkosh could meet the Street's quarterly expectation? Obviously, that's no way to run a business. And I would argue the stock *should* be worth less if the company was managed in such a way. Moreover, beyond the higher costs, the quarter was quite good, highlighted by strong sales and orders in Oshkosh's core construction equipment division.

Exhibit 3: Oshkosh Corp (OSK) Price Chart, May - August 2014

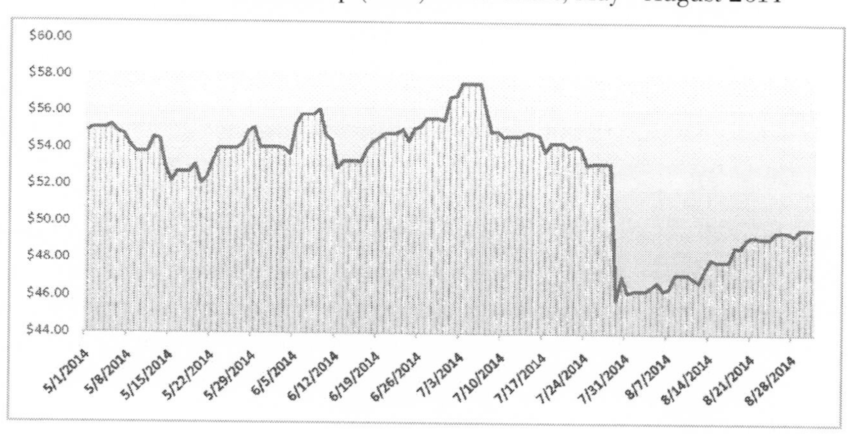

It is likely that the stock's large decline that day was accentuated because of "crowdedness" (hedge funds had lined up with the same long position). Also, it possibly served as a reminder to investors of previous disappointments made by the company, which mainly related to its Defense group. Regardless, it proved to be a buying opportunity (a term I typically resist saying because of its dramatic overuse on Wall Street and the almost never-quantified time frame given for which one can expect to capitalize on the "opportunity"), as the stock recovered much of that loss over the next month. Also, as foreshadowed by management on its second quarter conference call, Oshkosh's margins bounced back strongly in the following quarters. That allowed the Street to pay more attention to the continued positive order trends in its core business, ultimately sending the stock back close to its recent highs by the next spring.

Again, there are thousands of similar examples where the Street appears to put too much weight on what is likely a short-term issue, resulting in a dramatic move in a company's share price. Sure, skeptics might say unsignaled disappointments like this are a hit to management credibility or reduces, by at least some degree, the likelihood of the company meeting its earnings potential. Both of which could justify a lesser valuation for the company in the market, as a lower earnings multiple (e.g., PE ratio) might be warranted because of the greater uncertainty. Still, such occurrences frequently do not seem enough reason to cause a major move in a company's share price. Logically, other variables are often at play such as crowdedness, lopsided bullish or bearish sentiment going into an event, high short interest, dogpiling by sell-side analysts that change their rating after the announcement, or an unrealistic "whisper number." (That's another Wall Street term where I've become very cynical, as I'm convinced there is typically much less consensus "*whispering*" going on in most stocks than the financial press tends to convey. Moreover, the whispering that is reported frequently seems crafted in hindsight to explain a stock's performance.)

Contrarian Investing

With an exaggerated move in a company's share price either over a day or several weeks, the opportunity for savvy investors becomes taking the unpopular position opposite to the current sentiment. If one believes that the company's intrinsic value has not significantly changed, then he or she should have faith that other investors will similarly recognize the mispricing and the stock will *ultimately* correct back in line or closer to its original level. In hindsight, taking such a position counter to the mood of the day may seem like a very rational and easy decision. But, at the time, it's often a decision filled with doubt and uncomfortableness.

"*Cognitive Dissonance*" is the psychological term for this uncomfortable feeling. You may remember studying about it in an undergraduate Psych 101 class. I have long forgotten the textbook definition, but I think it is best described as basically going against the current, or the feeling you would have if you showed up at a black tie cocktail party wearing a swimsuit. In short, it's an awkward feeling we would strongly like to avoid.[2,3]

In the stock market, an individual who makes an investment in a dissident manner is typically dubbed a "contrarian," which has a simpler definition as "a person who takes an opposite or different position or attitude from other people."[4] I've found that contrarians are often some of the brightest players in the business, especially those who have diligently done the work that results in a thesis counter to Street expectations or the current sentiment surrounding a stock. It's a very rewarding position when one is correct. The contrarian feels as if he or she has beaten the game by not falling into the trap of the common investor that simply went along with the analysts' recommendations or the general emotions of the day.

Though for much of the time the investment is held, the contrarian stance is marked by loneliness, disheartenment, and doubt. No one wants to hold on to a sinking ship. And the fear of doing so tends to grow the longer the contrarian position is held without yielding results or confirmation that the consensus-opposing viewpoint has validity. Unfortunately for the contrarian, the constantly-quoted market price really provides too much feedback, which can lead to an unhealthy state of questioning and doubting the underlying thesis with every stock price move in the unintended direction. That in turn promotes more short-term thinking and often poor decisions. Trust me, I've been there.

The market preys on investors with weak conviction, those who need their ideas to be respected and confirmed by the daily price action. Unfortunately, it doesn't work that way. With a contrarian position, one must be prepared to deal with negative short-term feedback from the market. This is one reason I joke with my private equity friends that their job should be essentially stress-free, since there is no running scoreboard for them to constantly gauge their success. In fact, at times when I have held a strongly contrarian position, I have even wished that trading in the stock could be halted for some number of weeks or months and then resume hopefully at a price that better reflects my stance. This would be much preferable than receiving the daily pounding of negative market feedback and having to answer to a potentially doubting boss on why my thesis on the position still holds.

In essence, holding a contrarian position frequently feels like the equivalent of sitting outside while the big party inside is going on. An example that comes to mind is the bearish position many have had in recent years toward the electric car maker, Tesla Motors (NASDAQ: TSLA). Bears have regularly cited the lofty valuation of the stock, which came as its market capitalization quickly eclipsed that of many major automakers despite Tesla producing much fewer vehicles. They have also pointed to significant headwinds they expect the company will face, such as the high cost of battery replacement impeding new buyers from making the initial purchase. Finally, some who have been bearish on oil prices took the stance that Tesla's growth will be slowed by less urgency to make the switch to electric cars by consumers paying lower prices at the pump.

While these points may have seemed like valid issues, being on the short side of Tesla has been a tough place to be for most of the time in recent years. In fact, from the beginning of 2013 to mid-2015, Tesla's stock rose over seven-fold from roughly $35/share to a whopping $268/share. During much of this time, the number of TSLA shares sold short exceeded 25% of its share float. Hence, there were plenty of investors who bet against TSLA and paid a large price.

I've heard the investment case calling for shorting Tesla in much greater detail. It has been supported by fairly logical points in my view. Nevertheless, even with high convictions, many Tesla bears ultimately could no longer take the pressure of the constant stock market reminder that they were on the wrong side of the trade and were likely to remain on the wrong side for some unquantifiable amount of time. In many cases, this pressure to cover their short position was being primarily applied by risk officers or exasperated bosses at their funds. As economist John Maynard Keynes famously said, "The market can remain irrational longer than you can remain solvent."

Exhibit 4: Tesla Motors (TSLA) Price Chart, Jan. 2013 - Nov. 2015

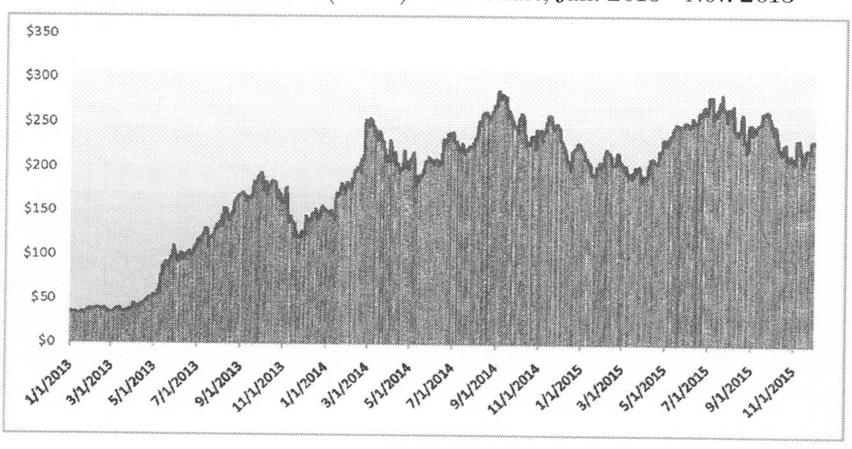

The opposite of the Tesla example would be for a company where sentiment is negative and the contrarian stance is to take a long position. Sometimes these situations are called "value traps," as the negative viewpoint remains the dominant thinking surrounding the stock and is frequently reinforced by the company's poor results. While sell-side analysts may still have favorable earnings outlooks for the company, investors heavily discount those forecasts by placing a low valuation multiple on the stock.

A stock that sticks out for me in this camp is Alcoa Inc. (NYSE: AA), the well-known global producer of alumina, aluminum, and aluminum-based products. Alcoa sat out much of the latest upcycle in the metals group. Instead, it spent the majority of the past decade disappointing the Street for various reasons including low aluminum or alumina prices, lofty energy costs, unfavorable currency effects, high start-up expenses, lackluster demand for some products, and just poor execution in general. Thus, with its frequent mishaps leading to downward estimate revisions by sell-side analysts, it was easy to be negative on the stock. And I was at most times. Alcoa was often my go-to short in the materials sector, as I felt confident the company had structural problems that would lead to even further disappointments. I slept well being short Alcoa and its management given their poor operating track record, as well as my investment track record of wining with a short position.

When I was short Alcoa, I still made it a point to understand the contrarian view, which was held mainly by investors new to the stock who had not experienced the time-after-time stumbles of the company. The contrarian bull case for Alcoa included the points that (1) aluminum had more price support than other metals since aluminum prices sat right above the global cost curve, or the price at which high-cost smelters would start losing money and, as a result, would at least theoretically cut production; (2) that Alcoa was replacing its high-cost capacity with new capacity in geographies with low energy costs like the Middle East; and (3) Alcoa's earnings from its engineered products segment would soon see a "lift off" given its high exposure to attractive end markets like aerospace. For those reasons and some others, analysts bullish on Alcoa tended to forecast outer year EPS in the $1.50-$2 range, despite the company consistently reporting quarterly earnings near or below breakeven. As such, stuck at $8-10/share or lower in recent years, Alcoa looked very cheap to those with such a favorable earnings outlook.

But again, the contrarian stance was a tough one. It received very little validation by Alcoa's quarterly earnings and certainly not by the typical earnings estimate downward revisions by sell-side analysts. Ultimately, many Alcoa bulls would finally lose patience with the poor execution and seemingly unreachable potential of the company and would abandon their long position.

Nevertheless, starting in early 2014, Alcoa's fortunes began to change, primarily the result of higher aluminum premiums (the amount the company could charge local customers above the quoted aluminum price on the London Metals Exchange [LME]). This caught many investors off-guard who were historically comfortable being short the stock, including yours truly and many of my experienced friends at other buy-side shops. At last, the contrarian Alcoa bulls had their relatively brief day in the sun, as the stock rose over 50% in the first three quarters of 2014. (It then subsequently fell back to prior levels largely due to the retreat in LME aluminum prices and regional premiums, as well as underperformance by the overall metals sector.) While it was still one of my worst trades that year, I covered my short position earlier than many of my peers who were reluctant to take a loss given their own experiences of winning with a short position. We'll later revisit this story as an example of the potential negatives of holding on to pre-existing biases due to past experiences.

Exhibit 5: Aloca Inc. (AA) Price Chart, Jan. 2010 - Nov. 2015

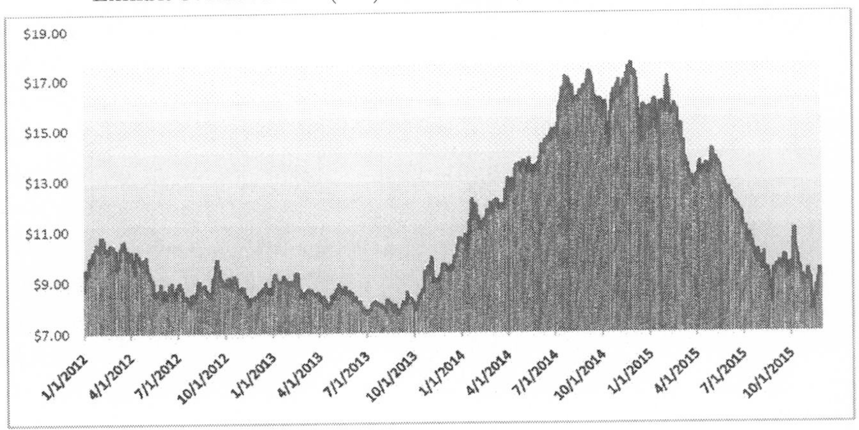

Not all contrarian positions are as difficult as these two. Still, it is unfortunately common that the portfolio manager or buy-side analyst who has crafted and best understands the thesis behind a contrarian idea is forced to abandon the position because of an anxious boss or risk manager who doesn't fully grasp (or care to grasp) the investment opportunity and is pressuring the PM to unwind the position since it is hurting the fund's overall short-term performance. Many firms are fine with their PMs making contrarian bets, but they unrealistically expect those ideas to work out relatively quickly and not hinder overall performance in the meantime. Sadly, those funds don't realize they can't have it both ways. They should either explain to their investors the patience required for taking contrarian positions and truly expand their investment time horizons, or they should just play the momentum game and cut off their underperforming positions quickly. Much of the problem is that managers at the same fund are often not on the same page as to which of these strategies their firm is actually pursuing.

Successful contrarian investing involves having a well thought-out thesis or belief why a stock has become mispriced. It is not taking a contrarian position just for the sake of being a contrarian. Unfortunately, this is a common tactic of many sell-side analysts in today's environment of heightened research competition. In recent years, the number of sell-side brokers has grown significantly from what was already a large base. One reason for the growth stems from personnel formerly at the major bulge bracket firms who left to form, or join, smaller firms due largely to the restrictions and limited research budgets at the big banks after the financial crisis. This undoubtedly has added to the preexisting research overcapacity among the sell-side, particularly as it relates to coverage of some larger companies. To illustrate, according to Bloomberg, there are currently a whopping 51 sell-side analysts that cover the stock of Apple, 52 for Facebook, and 46 for Amazon…just to name a few of the more popular stocks on firms' research coverage lists.[5] I'm all in favor of the existence of a wide variety of research and opinions being voiced among the investment community. But, does the world really need that many analysts covering the same company, providing largely similar forecasts, and commenting on the same data points…particularly if the analysts have the same viewpoint? (At this time, there are almost unanimously "Buy" ratings on those stocks.) I think most buy-side investors would unequivocally say "no."

Given this extensive competition, some sell-side research analysts feel like they need a nonconsensus outlook, rating, or point of view to stand out and be noticed by clients. Moreover, contrarian viewpoints can help generate votes for them in the annual *II* research survey. To quickly explain, *II* stands for the popular *Institutional Investor* Magazine, which for decades has ranked sell-side analysts covering the various sectors. The survey is highly important to many investment banks, who use high rankings to help pitch their services to potential corporate clients and to further justify research expenditures. As such, analysts are encouraged to make nonconsensus calls during *II*-voting season, as well as to visit clients more often and even send *II* trinket gifts that remind clients to vote for them in the survey. Somewhat embarrassingly, when I was an analyst following the environmental services sector, I sent clients a mini trash can to place on their desk that had my name and number on it and was filled with candy. (Fortunately, it wasn't a larger trash can or they might have thrown my research in it.) At least it wasn't quite as silly as a fellow analyst who made a music video regarding one of his stock picks. Needless to say, it did not get picked up by MTV.

It's all pretty ridiculous. Most buy-side clients couldn't care less about the rankings and view Wall Street's focus on the survey and the begging for votes as a waste of time and annoying. Moreover, the desperate attempts to gain the attention of buy-side clients via a contrarian call or other ludicrous measures highlights the research overcapacity that persists on Wall Street. It also does a disservice to the basis behind forming a true contrarian point of view.

On the buy-side, contrarian investors who seek a differentiated position without a solid reasoning or the work supporting such a position are easily shaken out when the price action doesn't quickly go their way and significant losses occur. Without high conviction in the idea, the pressure to unwind the contrarian position intensifies when the investing public's attitude toward a stock continues to drive momentum and valuation considerations take a back seat.

Instead, successful contrarian investing typically involves uncovering, understanding, and establishing strong conviction regarding one nugget of information that is incorrectly being priced by the market or a misguided belief that has overly influenced a security. It's been called having a "*variant perception*" by some value investors.[6] In fact, the term has been taken up as the moniker for a Boston-based contrarian investment group that offers investment advice based on data-driven, independent research that is professed to be a step ahead of the business cycle. I have never used their services, nor am I endorsing the group, but it sounds like the right approach to me.[7]

The nugget of mispriced information or the misguided belief can come in many forms. It can relate to the pricing of a good or a commodity, a trend in volumes, a critical cost item, or an industry dynamic, just to name a few. Naturally, some are more difficult to uncover than others, especially when it relates to a popular stock and when there are many other market participants also seeking the incremental information.

Much of my buy-side career has been spent analyzing commodities and commodity-related stocks. It's a sector where the largest stock performance driver is typically the commodity price itself. This makes uncovering the mispriced element frequently a challenge, particularly due to the overarching macroeconomic influences on commodity prices (e.g., value of the US dollar – since most commodities are priced in USD – and demand from emerging markets). In forecasting the price of carbon steel, for instance, I have often focused my efforts in determining the trends in scrap steel prices, which play a large influence on finished steel prices and which tend to move in very quick cycles. (At a conference I once attended, a private scrap steel dealer joked that he decided not to craft a presentation because it might be outdated by the time he arrived at the conference.) Staying on top of the swift pricing movements and nuances of the scrap market has frequently given me an edge in predicting future price changes for finished steel and in turn the direction of steel stocks. Nevertheless, at times, this edge has been negated by dominant macro issues, particularly since the value of the USD and overseas scrap demand (mainly from steel mills in Turkey) are the key determinants for US scrap exports and thus domestic supply. Moreover, whereas a decade ago I felt as if my scrap steel contacts were unique and proprietary, in recent years, it seems that more of my peers also have a Rolodex of industry contacts and similar ground-level access to information. Unfortunately, these factors have combined to somewhat diminish the ability to uncover the nugget of mispriced information by closely monitoring the pulse of the scrap market.

Still, this is not to say achieving the nugget of information on well-covered issues or something as popular as commodity pricing is unattainable. There are many situations that lend themselves to the potential to gain an edge if one is willing to go the extra mile to do the research. A supporting example comes from a former team member who did fabulous work in calling a decline in crop prices – particularly corn and soy – in 2014. In early summer of that year, my colleague took the initiative to take a trip to Iowa, visiting numerous farmers, ag processors, and grain storage providers.

He called me from the road saying, "Trip, I really think corn prices are about to get hit hard."

"OK, interesting. Sounds like you've had some good meetings then?" I replied.

"Yes, definitely. I've gained some great insight on conditions. I'll fill you in when I get back. But, in the meantime, let me make it simple for you. There is a saying up here of 'knee-high by July.' Take a look at the picture I'm sending you."

The picture sent from my colleague's phone was of him in the middle of a corn field with crops up to his waist. His trip was in mid June.

We had previously thought it might be a bumper crop at harvest later that summer, but his conversations in Iowa and, moreover his pictures, extraordinarily confirmed this expectation. The factors of high stocks (inventories) to begin the year combined with ideal growing conditions and new generation seeds were coming together to result in extremely well-supplied corn and soy markets. There was still an outside chance that adverse weather could turn things around, but given the existing inventories and likely record yields in upcoming months, a significant fall in corn and soy prices, as well as with most ag-related stocks, seemed inevitable. In the following weeks and months, my team member's assiduous efforts were rewarded as his bearish forecast proved correct in a big way.

Let me stop here and acknowledge that thus far I really haven't broken a lot of new ground. Such thoughts on working diligently to take a contrarian stance and having a variant perception have been written about and debated at length in many other places.

But, here is a point of view where I may differ and possibly offer some value-added thought:

It doesn't have to be so difficult! In my experience, many PMs and analysts believe the variant perception or an underlying thesis behind a trade has to be some sensational, CNBC-worthy event or uncovering that is almost entirely unique and not at all discounted in the stock price. According to that line of thinking, a contrarian approach on the short side means you have to believe the company is a fraud, that its products are obsolete, that its accounting is irregular, that its debt will swallow up the company, or that its sector will soon have a 2008-like crash. Or on the long-side, you need to find a completely hidden gem within a company or pick an inflection point at the very bottom of the cycle for the sector. Sure, those are all excellent reasons to have a contrarian position. But honestly, they don't come around with great frequency. And when they do, they often involve a company that is highly controversial, so the contrarian view may not be that unpopular after all since it is represented already by a large group of investors.

My key point here is that while the goal is still to work diligently to discover mispriced securities through a well-constructed thesis, you don't have to take on the world to win. For instance, I have had no opinion on the debate surrounding the nutrition and weight loss company Herbalife (NYSE: HLF) and the heated arguments on CNBC between notorious hedge fund titans Carl Icahn (a large Herbalife investor) and Pershing Square's William Ackman (a well-known hedge fund activist, who has had a large short position and calls the company a pyramid scheme). My only major takeaway after watching a rather entertaining clip of the two bad mouthing each other in front of a national TV audience in January 2013 (the brawl which some called "The Greatest Moment in Financial TV History") was that Ackman must have very differentiated insight on this company, or just extreme overconfidence, to give him this conviction or willingness to fight because there are certainly easier ways to earn a buck.[8] That's particularly the case if much of the investment community is gunning for you because they know you're short a large amount of stock and would like to force a short squeeze.

Exhibit 6: Exerts from CNBC Interview with Carl Icahn and Bill Ackman – January 26, 2013

Carl Icahn:

"Listen. You know, I've really sort of had it with this guy Ackman, you know."

"I'm telling you he's like a crybaby in the schoolyard. I went to a tough school in Queens you know and they used to beat up the little Jewish boys. He was like one of the little Jewish boys crying that the world is taking advantage of him..."

"He's the quintessential example of if you want a friend on Wall Street, get a dog."

"Listen to me... I want to say what I want to say and I'm not going to talk about my Herbalife position because you want to bully me...I don't give a damn about what you want to know. I want to talk about what I want to talk about...You can say what the hell you want. I'm going to talk about what Ackman just said about me, not about Herbalife..."

"I appreciate you calling me a great investor, but unfortunately I cannot say the same."

Bill Ackman:

"The big issue about Carl Icahn is he's not used to someone stepping up to him. Especially like me in 2003."

"What I thank Carl for is he helped highlight issues with Herbalife." [Ackman had accused Ichan of buying the stock and selling it.]

Source: CNBC.com

Going Where the Crowd is Not Focused

A much easier, less dramatic strategy seems to be concentrating your efforts in areas where others are not so focused, on stocks the brokers are not calling you about, on points no one seems to care about, and in cases where the Street's myopic short-term point of view is causing it to neglect a major issue just beyond the horizon. In essence, the aim is to find a contrarian point of view that may not represent an earth-moving discovery regarding a company, but just one issue not being given proper attention and not fully priced into the current stock price. These are ideas which probably lead to more singles and doubles in your portfolio rather than homeruns. But, I would contest going after such smaller victories is generally a more prudent way to run a portfolio than swinging for the fences. Moreover, some of the singles and doubles can turn into homeruns if your thesis continues to play out and you don't cash in too early.

Mispricing opportunities in the market tend to be most prevalent with smaller companies, which are generally characterized by relatively low market capitalizations and fewer average daily shares traded. With such stocks, there is typically less focus by Wall Street research and less widespread attainable thoughts on the company overall. I enjoy researching small- and mid-caps given the greater potential to uncover an important issue not already priced into the stock. One problem though if you're at a sizable fund is the illiquidity of many small-cap stocks and the resulting inability to deploy significant capital in those ideas. For instance, at my prior firm, I required a stock to trade a minimum of $10 million dollars per day in value to initiate a position. Otherwise, it was normally too difficult to get in and out of the position without significantly influencing the price. That was particularly the case if my targeted upside was as low say 10% (common for pairs positions), as I certainly couldn't afford giving up 1-2% when both initiating and exiting the trade. Fortunately, while I enjoy analyzing smaller companies, there are also many mispricing opportunities with larger-cap stocks, where the Street has simply taken the wrong focus or has overemphasized shorter-term issues.

So what's the genesis of such ideas? Where are good places to look?.. especially if you're wise enough not to blindly follow the advice of others, or if you're not just running preprogramed screens for ideas. The answer I believe is everywhere. Unfortunately, there is no single "idea well" providing an endless number of potential opportunities. Rather, you have to look for opportunities on a number of fronts. For me, I've tended to get my ideas from a wide variety of sources, as well as recurring tendencies for many stocks. Frequently, I've noticed an opportunity in a particular stock from my researching of another stock. And sometimes, I've been so wrong in my initial thinking that, after exploring the idea, I decided to take the opposite position.

Recurring Factors Leading to Significant Changes in Stock Prices

There are obviously many issues that can lead to a significant change in a company's stock price and that can be identified and capitalized on by hard-working investors and analysts. The following are some of the factors I've focused on to find ideas over the years. Importantly, the list is by no means comprehensive. A few are pretty obvious, and they certainly don't work on every occasion. Also, some are relatively minor issues that are unlikely to make the media headlines. But, in my experience, they have been recurring key catalysts or tendencies leading to a significant change in a company's share price, both in the short term and over time.

1) **Management is too optimistic.**

Nearly all corporate executives have invested huge amounts of time, energy, and personal wealth in their company. As such, it should come as no surprise that generally they are not the most objective sources when discussing the current conditions and prospects for their business. Management may well understand the stock market benefits of setting expectations low and then exceeding them. Still, they often just can't help themselves in communicating an overly confident and rosy outlook. They simply have too much invested not to have a very biased opinion. This also why they tend to take it personally when they somehow learn of investors who have sold short their stock. They see it as an insult to all their hard work and efforts to build the corporation. When I was a sell-side analyst, I remember traveling on a nondeal roadshow (a company's regular institutional investor meetings that are not associated with an upcoming share offering) with a

CFO who got extremely heated after learning that a person attending a group meeting was likely short their stock. I had to gently break it to him afterwards, "He wasn't the only one."

Management teams often don't seem to comprehend that a good company can be overvalued and thus be a good short, or that by shorting their stock, an investor may simply be hedging a bet on another company. For instance, in running a paired long-short book, I didn't need my short position to actually go down in price, but just to go up less than the stock I was long. I was amazed how many analysts I spoke with that couldn't grasp this concept. Moreover, management teams often fail to recognize that focusing on and possibly changing the minds of hedge fund investors who are short their stock can even lead to a "double buy" on the investor's part, as he or she buys the stock to cover their short position and then buys the stock again to go long.

One example of management's unavoidable optimism that comes to mind is my researching the stock of a small gold producer. At a conference, the CEO walked me through the history of the company and how he personally funded the initial capital of $10 million for exploratory drilling in Nevada. Talk about pressure. He had spent the vast majority of his wealth on digging holes in the desert. He admitted it was difficult to explain that to his wife. Fortunately for him, those drill holes led to the discovery of significant gold reserves and ultimately a producing mine for the company. He was a very interesting and knowledgeable executive. However, having risked so much and being so personally invested, I could quickly see how it would be hard for him not to have anything but an extraordinarily positive view of his company.

The opportunity with management optimism, either to short a stock or exit a long position, presents itself when that optimism is shared with the Street in investor meetings, earnings calls, conferences, and other forums. This in turn tends to result in overly aggressive expectations by analysts and throughout the Street regarding the company's earnings, cash flow, new developments, etc. By recognizing such optimism, investors are able to cash in (or avoid an unpleasant loss) when management ultimately concedes that it will not meet expectations.

Spotting aggressive expectations can be pretty easy. A good place to look is instances where analysts' estimates or company guidance calls for a dramatic jump in earnings, or where Wall Street research has an extremely positive outlook on a particular event that has been already conveyed by management. Also, in many cases, a company's promotional investor relations efforts results in a positive, well-received longer-term story that investors buy into. However, it also sets it up for near-term disappointments, as the company encounters bumps along the way.

2) **The earnings guidance trap.**

Whether to provide earnings guidance and what kind of guidance to give (e.g., quarterly or annual, EPS or operating earnings, a specific figure or a range) is often a dilemma for a company's management. Without formal guidance in accordance to the requirements of Reg FD, management cannot rein in sell-side analysts' earnings estimates that may be way off base. That in turn could lead to a large negative earnings surprise on the next quarterly reporting date. On the other hand, by providing earnings guidance, management often paints itself into a corner, particularly if industry or macro conditions are prime to change.

A given stock's reaction to an earnings disappointment or negative guidance by management varies dramatically. In today's market environment, stocks frequently go up on bad news because investors are already piled in on the short side, eliciting a short squeeze when they concurrently decide to cover. Therefore, when betting on an earnings miss or guidance shortfall, it's equally important to gauge sentiment and how broadly your expectation is shared by others. Honestly, my experience with quarterly earnings is quite mixed. I've often been frustrated when I was correct on the fundamentals, yet did not get paid for my work because investor positioning muted, or reversed, the expected stock price reaction.

I've tended to be a bit more successful when betting on annual earnings guidance, both to the positive and negative. To the positive, when industry conditions are favorable, a management team may enter the year with an overly optimistic view and thus give a rosy earnings outlook, which could boost the stock if it compares to the forecasts of more cautious or potentially doubtful analysts. In fact, some pundits have claimed that the tendency for management teams, and Wall Street in general, to be optimistic for the coming year, but then having to rein back that optimism as the year progresses is a key reason behind the market's strong historic seasonality of outperforming from November to May and underperforming in the summer and fall months. Thus, the old adage of "sell in May and go away" unsurprisingly coincides with the normal seasonality of negative earnings estimate revisions across the market.

Conversely, there are opportunities where the Street is caught with an overly optimistic outlook for the next year because analysts have not yet given proper focus on that period, even if they have reduced their estimates for the current year. Many times, analysts have yet to even break out their annual forecasts into quarterly estimates, and thus realize that their assumptions for the coming year are too aggressive. Also, sell-side analysts tend to base price targets on estimates for outer years. By keeping those estimates up, they can justify a higher valuation and a better rating on a stock they like. They can also possibly forgo having to downgrade a stock because of poor results and a lower earnings forecast for the current year.

However, where the rubber hits the road is when a cautious (and probably prudent) company management team takes a more conservative stance toward the coming year and gives initial guidance that is well below the average held by analysts. In some cases, it is just management hoping to set a low bar that they can beat throughout the year. But, in other instances, there exists an issue not fully understood by the Street that is the basis behind management's more cautious stance.

3) **Operating leverage larger than the Street perceives.**

Operational leverage is the magnitude of the change in a company's earnings given a change in its revenues. This one is a bit more complex, but may be my favorite factor to exploit, mainly since the Street often underestimates the degree of operational leverage inherent with many companies. By maintaining an earnings model for a company or studying sell-side analysts' models, one can get a better feel for a corporation's operational leverage and thus possibly gain a competitive advantage over those who have not done such analysis. In doing the spreadsheet work, I frequently have derived an earnings estimate that was substantially different than the Street consensus because my model accurately accounted for the large operational leverage of the company.

Operating leverage from pricing is most obvious since 100% of the rise or fall in revenues from a realized price change drops to the bottom line. There are generally no added costs a company incurs by raising prices. Depending on the size of the increase, production levels, and the financial leverage (debt levels) of the entity, the earnings impact from a price hike can be dramatic. For instance, let's consider a corporation with high operational leverage like US Steel (NYSE: X). If the company recognizes a $20 per ton increase in the price of flat-rolled carbon steel on its roughly 20 million tons of effective capacity (under full utilization), the operating earnings boost would be $400 million ($20 per ton on 20mt). That is the same as the full revenue increase, assuming the price hike was not driven by higher operating costs. On a full year basis after taxes, that would equate to roughly a $2 benefit to US Steel's EPS, a dramatic boost considering its earnings base in recent years. The frequent large pricing swings for steel and the large operational leverage for US Steel are key factors to the stock's high volatility. Unfortunately, this large operating leverage naturally has the opposite effect when prices decline. In summary, by correctly estimating the direction and magnitude of an upcoming price change for a company, one might derive a much differentiated view of its earnings prospects.

When it comes to volumes or activity levels, high operational leverage exists for companies that have substantial fixed costs. Those are costs that are unrelated to changes in volumes. My wife's yoga studio is a good example. Regardless of attendance, we pay teachers a flat rate per class. Our rent is a set amount. Our utilities are also largely fixed. So there are very few costs that we incur when an additional person takes a class. Essentially all of the revenues from that added person fall to the bottom line.

This is also the case for many manufacturing companies that are not operating at full capacity. In those cases, another unit is frequently able to be produced without adding more labor, overhead, or production capacity. By understanding and modeling out the high margins from the added volume, one can often derive earnings estimates that are more precise than analysts who are not giving proper focus on the incremental margin impact.

4) **Unrealistic expectations surrounding a new project or product.**

In the same vein as overly optimistic earnings outlooks by management teams, executives are often way too giddy regarding new projects or new products being introduced. The mining sector provides many examples, where a new mine start-up was much more problematic than originally expected. In analyzing the sector, I did not need to be a geologist or plant engineer to know there would likely be something significant that ultimately would go wrong when a mining company began to build or start up production at a new mine. The reasonings for the shortfalls were numerous and some quite amusing. They included everything from unexpected rock hardness (sounds like an oxymoron), to water leaks in underground mines (most notably, at a few uranium mines that were built *under* lakes. Now how could have that been a surprise?), to an actual wolverine who rummaged through the kitchen at an Artic mine of Agnico Eagle and was blamed for a large fire which closed the mine (I'm not making this up), to people in a residential neighborhood near a large new open-pit mine in Canada who complained about the noise. ("Hey, can you keep it down over there? [response] "Well, we *are* crushing rocks. Hard to do that silently, eh?").[9] The examples are endless. The clear opportunity is to bet against optimistic managements that are about to embark on a new project or a new product rollout.

Such aggressive optimism isn't attributable to only company management though. The financial press and investing public can also generate large enthusiasm and in turn a very high bar relating to a project or product. One example over the past decade was the introduction of Boeing's 787 Dreamliner plane. Plans for the state-of-the-art aircraft, which is considerably lighter than prior models because of advanced lightweight materials, initially received frequent hype by the press and analysts while customers waited for the first planes to be produced and delivered. However, the initial production of the plane was bogged down by major issues from subcontractors in addition to numerous safety-related delays in the certification process. The production timeline, as well as program costs, therefore had to be frequently revised to the negative. Largely due to the media hype and high expectations by Wall Street for the new type of aircraft, these announcements had a recurring negative impact on Boeing's share price, as well as that of some of its suppliers. (I would note that the initial headwind of the 787 ultimately turned into a tailwind for the company further into the product roll-out.)

5) **Management incentivized to beat expectations.**

Opposite to the potential for a company to disappoint, management may conversely be incentivized to beat expectations. This often occurs when there is a new management team in place that would like to start off on a positive note or if a company does not want to disappoint investors after a recent capital raise. Also, management may have expiring stock options priced at a level where positive news or results may be needed to attain that price. Finally, some management teams who are frustrated by critics of the company may go out of their way to announce favorable results or make positive comments to try to squeeze the shorts.

6) **Stale estimates.**

There are times when it becomes obvious to investors who are doing their work that some sell-side estimates for a particular company are stale. As silly as it seems, the eventual estimate adjustments and resulting change in the consensus figure, as well as potential ratings upgrades or downgrades, can have an impactful effect on a company's stock price.

7) **The Street is poised to miss an inflection point.**

An easy forecasting method is simply to assume a trend will continue without considering the possibility of a turning point that could change the fortunes of a company or industry. By seeking to identify specific catalysts, one can detect potential inflection points that others may miss.

The US corrugated container, or cardboard box, industry has been a good recent example. For many years, the industry was plagued by overcapacity and lackluster demand, resulting in dismal pricing. However, critics of the industry were caught off guard when aggressive industry consolidation and stronger consumer demand following the financial crisis led to a series of aggressive price increases in 2010-2012 that significantly boosted the earnings and stock prices for producers. Because their forecasts and views were based on rearview mirror analysis, many analysts and investors missed this key inflection point for the industry.

8) **Sentiment is turning.**

The beginning of a change in sentiment is frequently quite subtle. It can start with a slight positive announcement by a company, an analyst upgrade, a favorable development with the overall sector, a management change, the first quarter of exceeding Street expectations, or one upbeat comment by management on a conference call. Being in touch with sentiment and changes in attitudes is often critical in determining the right time to initiate a position.

How do you get in touch with sentiment? One way is to watch how the stock trades in reaction to important news and at certain price levels. Also, simply talk to people... analysts, salespeople, traders, your friends at competing firms, reporters, your parents that watch CNBC at 100 decibels, or just about anyone who has an opinion. Just remember that your objective is to determine sentiment and changes in sentiment, not to be overly swayed by the thoughts of others.

9) **A macro trend impacting several industries.**

The ultimate investing opportunity can be to capitalize on a major theme that has implications across several sectors. For instance, lower natural gas prices have had a clear positive effect on US ethylene producers, who mainly use natural gas liquids (NGLs) as feedstocks rather than naptha (an oil-based derivative), which is used largely by foreign producers. On several occasions in recent years, this advantage has provided a well-known benefit to the earnings of those companies. But maybe less obvious has been the benefit of lower natural gas costs on other manufacturing businesses, like the production of fertilizers or floor tiles that are also heavily reliant on natural gas.

10) **Operating problems that are likely recurring.**

Many problems at companies don't go away overnight. Rather, the first mention of an issue is often not the last, even if the problem doesn't crop up again immediately in the following quarter. Engineering and Construction companies (E&Cs) are notorious for this by announcing and taking a charge for a troubled project in a quarter, then having to take another large charge in a later quarter when they realize the project is even more distressed and costly than originally thought. This also happens frequently among manufacturing companies with a new plant start-up, where the initial inefficiencies and high costs are more persistent than expected.

11) **A minority part of the company isn't receiving enough attention.**

Companies are typically classified according to their main line of business. As such, the Street often neglects a smaller, yet important, segment of the corporation which could be a significant driver to earnings and valuation. I once followed the stock of a local Dallas-based public company, named Elcore Corp (later Elk Corp), which was a good example. Prior to its acquisition by GAF in 2007, Elk was by itself a major US player in residential shingles. However, the company also had a smaller technologies group that principally applied conductive metal coatings to plastic components within cellular phones. Natural fit, right?...shingles and cell phones. Maybe only logical if one's phone reception is so bad that they must get on their roof to make a call.

In any case, the corporation was typically labeled a building products company since the vast majority of its revenues came from shingles. Even during the technology bubble, Elk would typically present at what was perceived as boring housing and building products conferences, despite much of their presentation fitting the popular topic on Wall Street at that time. It was obvious to many investors (and I'm sure many investment bankers also) that a potentially highly-valued, sexy technology business was being hidden within a much less exciting building products company. Thus, there appeared to be a tremendous opportunity to create value through a sale or spin-off of the technology business, or even simply a corporate rebranding. Over time, this potential became more recognized and substantially benefited the overall valuation of Elk Corp despite the segment only accounting for roughly 10% of total company revenues. Unfortunately, the bursting of the tech bubble negated much of that value creation opportunity. Still, investors who recognized the potential hidden value prior to that time were rewarded.

12) **Opportunities for corporate action.**

You don't have to be a special situations analyst to identify companies that could receive a boost by announcing some sort of corporate action, such as a divisional spin-off, share repurchase plan, takeout, or that an activist shareholder has initiated a stake in the company. Sometimes the potential for such activity represents a cheap call option with a stock, while with other instances the opportunity is already reflected through a high valuation. The key is identifying such potential activity before the idea becomes mainstream and part of the consensus thinking for the company.

13) **A high or low bar going into an event.**

In many cases, one can simply look at a company's stock chart and tell if it faces a high or low bar going into an event. Naturally, companies with stock prices near their highs tend to have lofty expectations placed upon them and thus are faced with the onus of proving why they deserve their high valuation. Conversely, it seems at times that management of companies that have underperforming stock prices, and often a high short interest, merely just have to show up for an earnings conference call for the stock to go higher. Net-net, this isn't rocket science. The price chart itself can tell you a lot about the risk/reward of holding the position into an event.

14) **Management trying to hide a negative issue with a positive announcement.**

A seasoned sell-side analyst recently told me, "I think I may start to downgrade any company that announces a new cost-cutting program. It's so frequently a sign that there is a major issue that needs to be covered up." The same could be said for other types of positive announcements like a new stock buyback authorization (which doesn't necessarily mean the company is actually going to follow through and repurchase its shares), an acquisition, or a strategic alliance. At times, these announcements are made to take focus off a significant troubling issue at a corporation.

15) **Consensus betting against a trend that is likely to persist.**

Mean reversion is one of the strongest and most consistent tendencies in the market. It's particularly a good strategy if there is a catalyst to reverse the trend. However, trends often continue for longer than expected, especially if it's driven by a fundamental industry change.

In many cases, Wall Street adopts a consensus stance calling for a reversal in the trend. However, betting on the continuation of that trend can be a profitable trade as the Street and investors are often too early in calling for the momentum to reverse.

16) **The Street is erroneously extrapolating a trend.**

To the opposite extreme, trends are frequently expected to carry on and are extrapolated based on little information or on insignificant data, often resulting in an illogical forecasted result. Such an example is what people have called the "Elvis Paradox." It has been reported that there were 170 people impersonating Elvis when he died in 1977. After his death, that number grew dramatically, reaching an estimated 85,000 by the year 2000. This equates to a 31% compounded annual growth rate. If one assumes that rate has been maintained and continues (on a much larger base naturally), in ten years from now, one in every four people in the United States will be an Elvis impersonator. Moreover, by 2043, everyone on the planet will be dressed as the King.[10] (Thank you very much.) That's over nine billion people with blue suede shoes, which seems a bit extreme.

In financial analysis, a less dramatic, but still significant, extrapolation might occur when an analyst tries to forecast a company's gross margin expansion. That margin may have grown to 20% from 15% five years ago. But, expecting that figure to expand at similar rate over the next five years may be a stretch, particularly if there are industry or company-specific constraints preventing such growth.

17) **Past biases are dominating thinking and potentially ignoring a change occurring.**

This one was referred to earlier as it relates to Alcoa. For years, being short Alcoa was the right move. So hedge fund PMs like me, relying on their prior knowledge of the company, got too comfortable with the short position and overlooked the fact that in 2014 a change had occurred (higher aluminum premiums and a lower cost base because of the retirement of high cost capacity). Although experience may be your greatest asset, it can hurt you if you don't commit to remaining on top of the events impacting a company and instead merely rely on your prior knowledge. At times, I've been caught boasting about how well I know a stock, only to be asked when I last went to see the company. "Oh, I just saw them. I toured that plant. It's was...wait, I guess seven years ago now." Conversely, I've felt at times that I'm more successful when dealing with a company that I've only recently began to research, where my ideas are more freshly-formed.

18) **Overreaction to an unexpected event.**

Sometimes even good companies get themselves into jams. Many of those have serious financial impacts and long-term repercussions, while others are manageable, one-time events. Such dilemmas can involve a wide-range of topics, such as a recall on a product, a major class action lawsuit, being in the crosshairs of regulatory agency (like the EPA), or simply a bad partnership. The opportunity for investors is when the market either overreacts or underreacts to the significance of the trouble.

How do you judge if it's an over- or under-reaction? You have to do the work. You have to know the issue and the company inside and out and have a perspective on the impact of the issue to the viability of the company. It's not about looking at one day's stock price move and saying, "That looks overdone." It's having high conviction that the move is irrational because you understand the issue and know the real story better than most investors.

19) **New information likely to be released or discussed.**

Events such as conference calls, investor conferences, or industry conventions are often forums in which companies release news or discuss new information. As such, they can serve as ether positive or negative catalysts for stock prices. Obviously, the critical point is doing the work to correctly identify the likely nature of the new disclosure and how it will be received by the Street.

20) **Fear is causing the market to misunderstand the situation.**

It's broadly recognized that fear and greed are the main psychological conditions that drive the market. Warren Buffet was the first to truly promote the idea and there has been little denial of it in the investing community since. However, according to Buffet in a 2011 interview with *Fortune*, fear is the more powerful of the two forces. "There is no comparison between fear and greed. Fear is instant, pervasive and intense. Greed is slower. Fear hits."[11]

Unquestionably, the presence of fear in the market can lead to large overreactions and unjustified securities prices in the minds of many. The opportunity for rational investors is to recognize when fear is distorting a situation and to take a position counter to the current sentiment (the essence of contrarian investing as discussed previously). A recent example of such an opportunity involved the spread of the Ebola virus that infected a few Americans in late 2014. The news item of primary concern related to a Liberian man who was infected in Africa, but was treated in Dallas. When he was hospitalized, he infected a couple members of the medical staff, which ignited hysteria among much of the public that the disease was now spreading among the U.S. population.[12]

The national media undoubtedly fanned the flames of this fear, essentially suggesting the situation could soon be out of control and that Dallas was on the verge of becoming "*The Night of the Walking Dead.*" This was despite the fact that the local "outbreak" was isolated to one host carrier who had given it to two members of the medical staff at one hospital…hardly an out-of-control situation. Still, fear was abound and the stock market quickly began to reflect that worry. Living in Dallas, I think I recognized the scope of the overreaction and misunderstanding held by much of the nation when Eli Manning, the quarterback of the New York Giants, said his team would still travel to Dallas to play the Cowboys on the coming Sunday since, "With what we are doing and where we're staying. I think we'll be fine."[13] It was then apparent to me that the pull-back in stocks because of the fear had provided a short-term opportunity in the market. This proved correct as the Ebola worries waned and the market recovered to prior levels.

Of course, there are times when legitimate fears and real risks in our world justifiably worry investors and thus cause market sell-offs. However, it is important to be able to identify and separate those real threats from time-to-time irrational panic. By doing this and maintaining a calm and questioning nature, we can use the fear to our investing favor.

Exhibit 7: Recurring Factors that Tend to Lead to Significant Price Movements in Stocks

1) Management overly optimistic
2) Earnings guidance mismanagement
3) Operating leverage larger than perceived
4) Aggressive expectations for a product or project
5) Management incentivized to beat expectations
6) Stale analyst estimates
7) Trend extrapolation, likely to miss inflection point
8) Sentiment turning
9) A macro trend impacting several industries
10) Operating problems that are likely recurring
11) A minority division not receiving enough attention
12) Potential corporate action
13) A high or low bar going into an event
14) Management trying to hide a negative
15) Consensus too early in betting against a trend
16) The Street erroneously extrapolating a trend
17) Past biases is dominating thinking
18) Overreaction to an unexpected event
19) New information likely to be released or discussed
20) Fear is causing the market to misunderstand the situation

"Ladies and gentleman, this is your stewardess speaking. We regret any inconvenience the sudden cabin movement might have caused. This is due to periodic air pockets we encountered. There's no reason to be alarmed and we hope you enjoy the rest of your flight. By the way, is there anyone on board who knows how to fly a plane?"

Elaine, Movie: Airplane

Chapter 3:

How to Bake the Cake

Blackwell has long been known for its good wrestling, much less so for its football. For some reason the water in my hometown just doesn't breed many successful teams on the gridiron. So winning seasons are fairly rare. In fact, winning games are fairly rare in many seasons. My sophomore year in high school was one of those seasons.

It was near the end of the season, our record was horrendous, and we were on the road facing one of the better teams in the conference. Nevertheless, our coach cooked up a motivating pregame pep talk that ended with him throwing the chalk against the chalkboard and yelling something like "Now, go kick some ass!!" With a big cheer and no hesitation, we sprinted out of the locker room and onto the field with great vigor and hope. Unfortunately though, that hope went down the drain pretty quickly, as the opposing team immediately returned our opening kick-off for a touchdown. So much for the inspiring pregame pep talk.

Fast forward three quarters, the score was 38-0 in favor of the bad guys. Not a big surprise, but once again our team and our coaches seemed pretty exhausted. I was playing running back when a second and long play was sent to the huddle. "Coach says just give the dang ball to Rodgers and see what he can get on the left." ...Wait a second. What?!! I looked over very confused to our coach on the sidelines, who had his head in his hands at that point. Were we just giving up? We had plays to run. We practiced them often. OK, sure, they weren't working so well once again.

But why abandon our playbook completely? We've got to have some game plan, right?

Needless to say, that play didn't go so well. And similarly neither does investing when you have no game plan or when, like my coach, you abandon your playbook when things are not going well.

In the previous chapter, we discussed the basic elements of contrarian investing and factors that often present opportunities to capitalize on a future price change in a security. In this chapter, we'll dig into the process of researching a new idea, as well as the methods to examine and review existing investments…in other words, how to develop a playbook and a game plan.

Our goal is to establish a ritual that determines, after thorough analysis, if an investment has a favorable enough risk/reward profile that makes it worthy of adding it to your portfolio. (By the way, I never understood why it's common to say risk/reward and not reward/risk. Maybe because it appropriately places a higher importance on focusing on the potential risk elements of an investment.) For those seeking to sound smarter, it's also been referred to as identifying securities that have asymmetric upside/downside. Either way you call it, the objective is to find ideas where you don't lose much if you're wrong, but there is the possibility for an outsized gain if you're right.

The key is the process and consistently following that process for each investment. It's being devoted not to cut any corners, even if you've already convinced yourself of the trade based on your preexisting thoughts and opinions. That's a common mistake. In many cases, an investor gets excited about a trade based on one factor he or she has uncovered and thus skips much of the other due diligence. This is understandable. Once you believe you are onto a good idea, there is often a large sense of urgency to initiate the trade before more investors become aware of your findings or begin to glean your understanding.

I strongly believe that there are typically just a few (or less) factors that will ultimately be the main drivers of a security's value. The countless other variables end up being fairly trivial in capturing major moves in the market price. But, the real problem surfaces when something goes wrong with the idea or when your main reasoning for the trade has not played out as you had hoped. Unless you've done the work to fall back on and have considered the risks, you're a little lost at that point. You must have a playbook or some sort of method on how to best evaluate and deal with the situation. And, if you're really nervous that a trade is about to get away from you before you've finished all your work, my suggestion is to initiate a small position and then build up the size of your holding as you do the work and if your analysis continues to support the position.

It's been said that the investment process is even more important than the actual result. I'll admit, I'm not willing to go that far. At the end of the day, the scorecard doesn't give style points, and the money made from a fortunate event is just as green as that made from an expected occurrence. **Still, the importance of having a process is that it simply increases your chance of success.** Just like the golfer with a pretty swing in most cases should outplay the hacker who may get lucky every now and then.

Consider the casino game of blackjack. It's not a difficult game to understand, but there are some scenarios where even seasoned players forget which decision has the highest chance of winning. Therefore, if you are not familiar with how to play the game or feel like you need to ensure you have the best odds, you should probably go to a gift shop near the casino and buy one of those little cards that gives instructions on when to hit and when to stay. (The dealer even normally lets you put the card on the table and refer to it if you are not too embarrassed to pull it out.) The makers of the card have already computed the highest probability of success for every situation you may be dealt. So, it's really an easy little playbook, which shouldn't be called into question. You can take comfort in knowing that if you are following the card, you are playing the game using the highest odds and can probably even enjoy a cocktail while you do so.

For instance, the little instruction card from the gift shop will say that if you are dealt two cards that sum to 16 and the dealer has a face card showing, you should always hit. No questions asked. The assumption is the dealer's hidden card is a seven or greater (a 61.5% chance in a multi-deck game), under which the dealer would be required to stay at 17 or higher and your 16 would lose. Even if you do as you should and hit, and then you lose because perhaps you got a face card and busted, you shouldn't complain. The highest probability to win was to hit. That's what the playbook said. You followed the process. Regardless if the dealer ultimately busted as well and you would have won if you had stayed on 16, hitting was still the correct choice. There is no benefit to second guessing or thinking "what-if." By following the predetermined process, you can look back at the result much more objectively and know that if you continue to play in such a manner, you will have the best odds for success.

There are two processes that are important to engage in when analyzing securities and running a portfolio. **First, you must have a process for analyzing new ideas. And, second, you must have a process for reviewing positions already in your portfolio, particularly when they are not going in your favor.** You may already have set processes for both of these. My goal here is just to emphasize the importance of the process, as well as review some key factors you may incorporate into your ritual. Again, this list of due diligence factors to consider is not exhaustive. There may be many other topics you need to explore or questions you should ask depending on the issues and circumstances of the potential investment.

Process for New Ideas

Let's start with new ideas. To gather information in my process, I typically use a number of sources, including company presentations; regulatory filings (e.g., 10Ks and 10Qs); sell-side industry and company reports (particularly initiation reports); industry association presentations; company conference calls; conversations with management, industry contacts, and analysts; media reports; and third-party research reports (such as *Seeking Alpha*, one of my favorites).

- ***Sector Issues.*** If I'm new to both the security and the sector, I generally start broad and then work my way down to the nitty gritty of the company. First, I look at the sector and factors such as the industry's growth prospects, cyclicality, barriers to entry, cost structure, pricing volatility and history, regulations, level of consolidation, exposure to macro risks, range of returns, and various operating strategies among participants.

  I then look at the company's position within the industry. Is it a high- or low-cost player? Does it have a high market share? Is it a price leader? Is it a consolidator? How do its products or services compare with the competition? Has it taken an innovative or unique approach relative to its competition? Again, these are just a few of the important questions you might want to explore.

- ***Earnings history and profitability.*** Next, I look at the company's earnings history and its profitability levels. What are the key drivers to its top-line growth? -- New products, gaining market share, sector volume growth, pricing? What drives its margins? Is it a high fixed-cost business? Does it have a high level of commodity or currency exposure? Is labor a big cost item? How variable (tied to volumes) are labor costs? Has the company incurred a lot of one-time expenses, such as start-up or product development costs, which are likely temporary? Is there any delay between costs and the related revenue recognition? What other items stand out on the company's income statement? Are SG&A costs as a percent of sales inflated or skimpy versus peers? If the company is leveraged, are interest costs a major item? Are they fixed-rate or variable? Is the company's tax rate likely over- or understated? Do book taxes differ materially from cash taxes? A lot of questions here, and again I'm definitely leaving many out.

- ***Capital Structure.*** Regarding the balance sheet, I first consider the company's capital structure. Has it become over-leveraged (taken on too much debt) at a poor time in the cycle? How much debt coverage does the company have (expressed by its net debt/EBITDA ratio)? Will it likely need to access the capital markets soon? What are its debt maturities? What are the trends in working capital? Does it have excess cash? Is its cash "trapped" in another country for tax reasons? Are there long-term assets that are undervalued on the balance sheet that would generate a significant gain if sold? Are there significant off-balance sheet liabilities that are generally unknown or potentially incorrectly valued (such as leasing obligations or conditional inventory at customers), information that typically has to be dug up in the footnotes of the regulatory filings.

- ***Cash Flow Outlook.*** Cash flow is particularly important with companies with high financial leverage, as investors want to know how fast debt levels can be reduced or managed. But, it's important to consider cash flows with any corporation, especially in analyzing how they compare to net income levels. Potential red flags should be identified with companies where operating cash flows have consistently fallen short of net income or where cash flows are reliant on one-time events, like asset sales. "Cash is king" and "Cash doesn't lie" are trite sayings, but are still vital to remember when doing cash flow analysis. Finally, it's important to determine the likely uses of a company's future cash flow (e.g., share buybacks, dividends, capital expenditures, acquisitions) and how the Street might possibly view such cash allocation.

- ***Management.*** Management is largely a subjective variable, thus making it not my favorite factor to analyze. One's assessment or "gut feel" for a management team after meeting with them once, or even many times, is often incomplete and may not be a fair representation of a particular executive's abilities to run the company.

Still, I've always believed a poor management team is the card that trumps all other factors. So assessing management is critical. One should look at how management is compensated. Are they significantly invested in the company and have interests that are aligned with shareholders? How did they rise to their position? Is their background in finance or law, or more operationally-focused? What is management's track record at the company or at prior companies? How do they interact with the board of directors? Is the board overcompensated or has it been stacked with puppet directors who will just go along with the chairman's wishes? What about other corporate governance issues? Is the CEO also the president or chairman?

Maybe most importantly, how is management viewed by the Street? Are they seen in a positive light by creating shareholder value, often exceeding expectations, actively addressing shareholder concerns, and being readily available to investors at conferences, roadshows, analyst meetings, and site tours? Or are they seen to have destroyed value, frequently overpromising, avoiding commenting on difficult issues, and poorly communicating with the Street? Investors' views of management can go a long way in explaining the valuation the market is placing on the corporation.

- ***Sentiment.*** Hand in hand with the Street's feelings for management is its sentiment toward the company's prospects in general. It's critical to assess if investors and analysts are heavily biased to the positive or negative. Look at the dispersion of analysts' ratings. For instance, if there are only "buy" ratings, who is left to upgrade the stock? Are the negative or uncertain aspects of the story being underrepresented in the market? Talk to both bulls and bears of the company to get both perspectives. Chat with salespeople, and particularly sector salespeople if possible, to assess the views of their other clients. Again, our goal is not to be overly influenced by the opinions of others but just to evaluate sentiment. Ask conference coordinators which companies were most heavily requested for management one-on-one meetings. Consider if the media has helped shape sentiment. Do stories exaggerate the positive or negative aspects of the company?

- ***Street Expectations.*** One should consider the potential for sell-side analysts' earnings expectations to be biased to the positive or negative, often depending on the guidance of management. In some cases, estimates can be stale, especially outer-year forecasts. Other things to analyze are a company's recent earnings revision history, the dispersion of estimates (which again could be due to some outdated estimates), its earnings surprise history, and the seasonality of earnings. For instance, if a company typically generates 55% of its earnings in the second half of the year, yet analysts are expecting 70% this year, then expectations could be too high. This often happens when a company misses expectations early in the year, but analysts, rather than lowering their full year estimate, just push out those earnings to their forecast for quarters later in the year. This could be possibly in efforts to maintain their annual estimate and price target.

Exhibit 8: Key Factors to Investigate with New Ideas

Key Factors	*Some Items of Focus*
Sector Issues	- Industry structure & growth prospects - Company's fit within industry
Earnings History and Profitability	- Key drivers to revenue growth - Main items impacting margins - Recent trend in earnings
Capital Structure	- Amount of debt on the balance sheet - Debt metrics & maturities - Off-balance sheet liabilities
Cash Flow Outlook	- How fast can the company delever? - How do cash flows compare to net income? - Planned uses of cash flow
Management	- Management background - Corporate governance issues - How is management viewed by the Street?
Sentiment	- What are the bull & bear cases? - What factors that have shaped sentiment?
Street Expectations	- Recent estimate revisions - What is the earnings surprise history? - Are estimates biased or stale?
Top-down issues	- What are the most important macro issues? - Will macro issues overshadow other factors?
Possible Corp Action	- Potential for activism & likelihood for success - Various options for the company
Key Risks	- What are the main risks? Is there "event risk?"
Shareholder List	- Characteristics of top holders; recent changes
Unique or Consensus? / Contrarian or Trend Following?	- Is it a contrarian idea? - How unique is my thesis ?
Technicals	- What are the main technicals to observe?
Valuation	- Key metrics, Is the multiple appropriate?
Catalyst	- What is my main catalyst? Is it well known?

- ***Top-down Issues.*** Apart from sector issues, it's important to identify which macro issues are most critical for the company. Major macro factors such as energy costs, the valuation of the US dollar, and consumer confidence can take precedence and overshadow sector or company-specific issues. You should consider if the stock has historically been driven by such overarching factors, often negating any bottoms-up research and making it more difficult to attain an edge in your analysis.

- ***Possible Corporate Actions.*** In today's environment of increased investor activism, this has become an even more important factor to analyze. Things for consideration here include: Is the company a consolidator or likely to be bought? Is there a potential divesture or segment that could be spun-out that could add value? Could the company decide to take on a major share repurchase program or pay a special dividend? Could it look at alternative tax strategies, like an MLP? Investors should also carefully ponder the likelihood of an activist to be successful in their demands. How difficult will it be to secure seats on the board? Are their proposals for change viable or realistic with market or sector conditions?

- ***Shareholder List.*** Take a look at the first few pages of the shareholder registry, which are updated quarterly. What type of investors constitute the shareholder base? Are the top-page holders largely hedge funds that are probably more temporary owners or are they longer-term holders like pension plans? What are the major changes in ownership from the prior period? Has the "smart money" (an example of self-labeling by hedge funds) been selling or adding to its holdings?

- ***Key Risks.*** Identifying the main risks is probably the most important part of any investment process. These risks could relate to a wide range of issues, such as regulatory actions, earnings, corporate activity, sector events, or analyst recommendations. Some of the risks may be inherent with the position and the timing is unknown. Conversely, there are other risks, like a company's quarterly earnings release or new information being given on its investor day, where the exact date is known and which are generally termed "event risks."

Investors should spend considerable time thinking about event risks and how it relates to a security. Do you have particular insight or strong conviction regarding the event? Is one side of the trade crowded so that if the expected outcome occurs, the response will be muted, or if the opposite outcome occurs, the response will be exaggerated? Has the price action in the security going into the event led to a high or low bar for management? In general, investors must simply ask themselves if holding the position through the event risk is really worth it. Tax implications aside, if one does not have strong conviction and if the potential reaction does not have a positive asymmetric risk/return profile, then unwinding or reducing exposure, and possibly reinitiating the position after the event, may be the best option.

- ***Unique or Consensus? Contrarian or Trend Following?*** Previously, we discussed the importance of realizing if your idea is unique or likely shared by the consensus. Is your thesis a contrarian idea or does it seek to capitalize on the established trend of the security? If it is a contrarian idea, you should consider what it would take to get others to come around to your thinking. What is the realistic time frame needed for that to happen?

- ***Technicals.*** I generally don't spend much time analyzing the trading patterns of stocks. But, it's worthwhile to at least be aware of some of the major technical issues, particularly if others are giving credence to these factors. Some of the basics here might include a stock holding its 200-day moving average or a stock selling off on days of large volume. Analyzing the technicals of a security may be especially helpful regarding the timing of when to initiate or trade a position.

- ***Valuation.*** I previously said I would not make this book overly academic. Thus, a long discussion of this topic would likely violate that promise. Undoubtedly, valuation is a critical element to consider in the investment process, be it the standard measures such as EV/EBITDA, PE, Price/Revenue, Price/Book, dividend yield, etc., or sector-specific ratios like Price-to-Clicks for internet marketers or cap rates in real estate markets. My main point of caution is to remember that valuation can be more art than science. Much of the time, it encompasses large subjectivity. For instance, when I was a sell-side analyst, we were required to make a brief presentation to an internal research committee when we wanted to change a rating or initiate coverage of a stock. Several times the committee would ask me "What does your DCF (discounted cash flow) analysis tell you?" And I would answer, "It tells me whatever I want it to." That may have been an arrogant response, but it was true. As anyone who has done DCF analysis can attest, a slight tweak in the variables, like the discount rate or the terminal multiple, can have a dramatic impact on the final valuation. So with small changes, I could achieve essentially whatever price target I desired.

My other word of caution here relates to value traps, where low earnings ratios look too good to be true. Many times they are, as it becomes apparent that the estimated E (earnings) in the P/E ratio is too aggressive. Moreover, in times of distress, the E often declines faster than the share price, making a once cheap stock now look expensive even after it has fallen. Getting too hung up on valuation multiples can be a costly mistake if you have not done proper due diligence on the likely direction and the magnitude of change in earnings. Growth stocks that seem expensive may be less so if earnings rise greater than expectations, and stocks that seem cheap may later prove pricey when estimates fall.

- ***Catalysts.*** Especially for contrarian ideas, one should identify catalysts that will result in the idea being discovered or at least getting more attention. A catalyst could be the same event risk identified above, but one in which you have considerable conviction and a favorable risk/reward scenario. It may be a company-specific catalyst, a sector catalyst, or a macro-related catalyst. Regardless, it is important to determine how widely-shared your catalyst is and to gauge the level of investor crowdedness relating to the event. Many times, I've been disappointed with the response to an event, like an earnings surprise, as I had not properly evaluated the popularity of my position and the catalyst.

- **News flow.** It's important to anticipate the news flow when deciding to initiate or add to a position. You should consider that if a company's recent news flow has been poor, is there a reason to expect it to improve? Does management need to come clean on any important issues? Is there a critical industry factor that that the company has not yet addressed? Or could there be a possible upcoming news item that might favorably impact sentiment? Is management motivated to announce positive developments? Alternatively, is the company at a stage where news flow is likely to be more negative?

An excellent trade example of anticipating news flow comes from the gold industry, and relates to management's tendency to be overly optimistic on a new project, but later having to face the music when disappointments occur during the construction and initial production stages. In 2012 through early 2013, Osisko Mining Company and Detour Gold (TO: DGC) were very similar in that they both had one large Canadian project that constituted the vast majority of the value of each company. However, the timing of development for the projects differed. For Osisko, its Canadian Malartic project had just recently reached commercial production, having already past the periods of its initial drilling, feasibility studies, and construction. Conversely, Detour's project, Detour Lake, was still delineating its resource and preparing its feasibility study. At this stage, it was likely that the drilling results and feasibility details that Detour chose to release to the public were going to be favorable, shedding positive light on the project. Management was incentivized to release positive updates, particularly with the need to possibly access more financing to construct the project.

On the other hand, Osisko was in the more difficult initial start-up phase at Canadian Malartic. Thus, its news flow was more likely to be negative, reflecting the normal start-up challenges with any large project. Therefore, by going long Detour and short

Osisko at that time, one could hedge out the impact of the gold price and isolate the vastly different expected news flow among the two companies.

A likely better-known and more recent example of the importance of anticipating news flow relates to Chipotle Mexican Grill, Inc. (NYSE: CMG) and the contraction of the E. coli virus by some of its customers. When the unfortunate occurrences were first announced in October 2015, one could have correctly deducted there would be more negative developments and news stories about the issue in future months. Therefore, even if an investor had a positive take on the company beforehand, it should have been clear the issue was likely going to provide for substantial news headwinds for the stock in the near term.

- ***What's the right size?*** Once you've decided that a security has the merits for your portfolio, you should address the question of sizing. What percent of your portfolio should the position represent? If you've done the work and believe the idea is compelling, it should be large enough to compensate you for your time. On the other hand, as possibly prohibited by your firm's investment restrictions and risk policies, you probably don't want to bet the farm on any one idea.

The first step in determining the adequate size of a position is setting guidelines for the range of position weightings within your portfolio. As an example, I have typically used a range of 2.5%-8%, with an average position being roughly 5% of my book. This particular sizing equates to approximately 20 positions in the portfolio. Granted, this could be greater-than-desired concentration for some portfolios. Still, the number of my positions has tended to vary substantially depending if I have several older and smaller positions that I am in the process of exiting. As a general rule, once a position is only 2.5% of my portfolio, the next unwind is a complete exit. My reasoning is that it is not worth my time to manage positions that are smaller than this, as they begin to have little consequence to the performance of the entire portfolio.

With the range of position sizes in mind, I then have used four factors in determining the appropriate size of a particular trade: liquidity, volatility, expected upside, and conviction level.

(1) ***Liquidity*** - Naturally, if you are managing a significant amount of capital, less liquid positions necessitate a smaller size in your portfolio since it is more difficult to put money to work in these trades, as well as to exit if something goes wrong. Smaller portfolios that can easily get positions on and off "the sheets" (the portfolio) may be able to ignore this issue.

(2) ***Volatility*** - Highly volatile positions also have tended to have a lower weighting in my portfolio. It's easy to comprehend that maintaining large positions in highly volatile securities elevates the standard deviation of returns with the overall portfolio. This in turn increases the required return of the portfolio, since many investors critique a PM's performance by his or her *Sharpe Ratio*, commonly defined as the portfolio's real return divided by its standard deviation. Developed by William F. Sharpe in 1966, the Sharpe Ratio is a rather simple formula that measures performance by accounting for how much risk a PM assumed in order to generate the portfolio's return.[1] Thus, as illustrated by the formula below, positive returns with highly volatile stocks can generate a lower Sharpe Ratio, and thus be viewed inferiorly to lesser returns generated by lower beta securities. Admittedly, the basic Sharpe Ratio is criticized for several shortcomings, most notably the assumption that risk equals volatility, and that all volatility is bad and should be treated the same. Again, I'm not going to debate the academic strengths or weaknesses of the ratio here. Rather, I'm just pointing out that it is a frequently-used measure to judge PMs and that it should be considered when evaluating the risk-reward tradeoff in a portfolio.

Exhibit 9: Basic Sharpe Ratio Definition

Sharpe Ratio = $(Rp - Rf) / \sigma p$

Where:
Rp = Portfolio return
Rf = Risk free rate
σp = Portfolio Standard Deviation

Source: Investopedia

(3) ***Expected upside*** - After consideration of the two factors above, positions which have the largest estimated upside should typically have higher weightings in the portfolio. This is pretty simple. To maximize your overall return, your main pay-off pitches should be appropriately sized in your book.

Exhibit 10: Key Factors to Determine Position Size

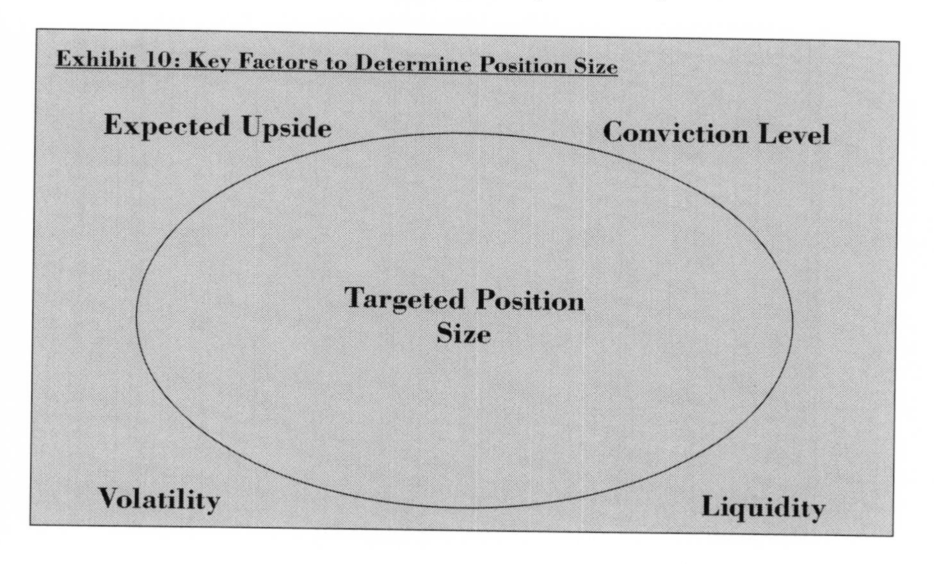

(4) ***Conviction levels*** – Finally, of course, you should be overweight positions where you have the greatest confidence. Unfortunately, this factor is less quantifiable that the other three. Still, when entering into a new trade, I try to judge my conviction level

relative to the other positions in my book and use that comparison as a guide based on my average position size in the portfolio.

- ***Have a Game Plan.*** Before you initiate a position, you should think about how you might trade the position. Under what conditions will you add or unwind? And how large will those trades be? Should you hedge the entire trade or elements of the position? (That is if you are not required to do so already under your fund's mandate.) How might you trade the position around event risks?

A worthwhile practice is to attempt to budget and map out how you are going to make the most dollars out of the trade. After all, we are really after dollar gains, not percentage gains. Percentages don't pay for your kid's education or your next vacation.

For instance, let's say you have a $10 million dollar position with an estimated base case return of 20% and a forecasted risk scenario of -10%. Therefore, your estimated upside-downside is 2:1, and you believe the upside has a higher probability of occurring than the downside. Naturally, if you hold the entire position until it hits your target of +20%, you will make $2.0 million. That's a great scenario. However, in many cases, stock performance is not linear and the road to up 20% may be choppy, providing opportunities to add or unwind part of the position and even make more than $2.0 million if traded well. Also logically, you may decide to take off half of the trade at say +10%, as the risk/reward tradeoff at that price seems more balanced and doesn't support holding a full position. This would be a safer play, but would result in you making only $1.5M if your target was ultimately reached with just half your original investment ($1 million made on the original $10 million after the first 10% return plus another $500k made on $5 million after the second 10% return).

There are countless scenarios, yielding a wide range of returns. It is not crucial that you consider all of them, but it is important when you initiate a position to establish price targets of where you would expect to add and where you might unwind. For instance, a position that represents 5% of your portfolio might be worth expanding to 7% if it declines 5% from your entry point. Similarly, it might be worth reducing to 3% if climbs 10%.

I strongly believe there should not be uniform add/unwind parameters that are used across the portfolio. Such levels should be specific to the volatility and estimated upside for each position. For a trade that has 10% upside, unwinding some of the position when it is up 5% may be prudent. But, for a position with 20% or greater upside, it's probably too early to take that initial trade. It's simple math that your overall return will be substantially greater the longer you can maintain a full position and hold out on unwinding your winning trades (i.e., letting your winners run). **The main point here is not to map out each scenario, but to have a predetermined idea of how you might trade the position rather than making decisions on the fly or based on your emotions of the day.**

Process of Portfolio Maintenance

Many PMs spend too much time shopping for new names to add to their portfolio versus continuously examining and questioning their existing positions. Reviewing your current trades and rehashing your outlook for each position is generally not as invigorating as finding new ideas. **However, keeping on top of the relevant issues with your book and even growing your conviction levels are paramount to successful investing.**

A key element of portfolio maintenance is keeping tabs on the main factors that led to your investment in the first place. You should regularly review the items in your due diligence process (such as the factors we discussed earlier) and continuously update your work on earnings models, investment write-ups, and presentations. Staying current on a position means to diligently remain in contact with industry sources, management, and analysts and to continuously question if your investment thesis still holds or has even been strengthened, possibly making a case to increase the size of the position.

PMs should continue to evaluate catalysts for the position and sentiment toward those catalysts. If one of your main original catalysts was that earnings expectations for the upcoming year were too high, and now Street estimates have dropped with no reaction to the stock, it is likely worthwhile to consider whether there is still a valid reason to hold the position in your portfolio.

Similarly, PMs and analysts should review and update their base, best, and risk targets for the position, particularly if their earnings estimates have changed. A stock that has experienced falling estimates may now have to realize an unrealistic multiple expansion to hit your prior price target. Alternatively, rising estimates may now make your prior risk case scenario appear too dire.

One practice I have performed weekly, or sometimes daily, with my portfolio is ranking my positions by conviction level. My rankings have tended to change fairly frequently, and I have had to be careful not to let emotions get involved by automatically ranking frustrating positions at the bottom of the list. Nevertheless, the practice of ranking has tended to help me maintain appropriate sizing and has forced me to establish a regular process in reviewing my thoughts on the positions in my book.

Common Pitfalls

Investors needs to be aware of some of the common mistakes in maintaining a portfolio. Here a few of those that I have found my portfolio at times to be most susceptible:

- **The Endowment Effect.** This is simply being biased to hold on to a position because it is already in your portfolio. Under the Endowment Effect, our perceived value of something is greater because we already own it.[2,3] PMs too often feel an emotional attachment to their positions as if when they initiate a trade, they are driving off the lot with a new car that cannot be returned. In fact, studies have shown that if PMs were forced to unwind their entire book and then reinvest all the money the following day, many would not reinitiate the same positions. Absent high trading costs or illiquidity, this seems quite irrational. The reality is PMs should approach each day as a clean slate. Every position has to earn its right to stay in your book everyday regardless of your history, knowledge, or prior conviction level with the investment. As I've frequently told members of my team, "These are stocks, not our children." You have be open to the possibility that a stock you loved yesterday may be one that you should sell today.

- **Making the same bet across the portfolio.** It is important to realize if a number of your trades share a common theme, which dramatically increases the correlations across the positions in your book and can lead to some large swings in your returns. Examples are having a shared long bias to oil prices or a short bias to the US dollar or interest rates.

- **Unintended bets.** Often investors don't realize the unintended bets they are making that may overshadow their main reason for holding a position. For instance, at times I've owned shares of CEMEX (NYSE: CX), the global cement producer, because of my favorable outlook on the cement industry or construction trends in its operating regions, particularly the United States. However, representing 7% of the Mexican Bolsa exchange, Cemex also trades with a high correlation to its home stock market, even with the vast majority of its liquidity being with its US-listed ADR. This has made the stock at times more of a play on the country of Mexico in general than the cement industry.

- **Don't be "a dick for a tick."** I didn't make this one up. It's a well-known saying emphasizing not to be so picky on your entry points when initiating a trade that you miss getting the position in your portfolio. All too many times, I have been too stubborn to pay up a little for a stock, only not to have enough money invested in the position when my catalyst comes to fruition and the trade performs as I had hoped. There's nothing more frustrating than being right, but not making much money.

- **Nothing working.** If you are too quick to unwind your winners and continue to add to your losers, you will naturally end up with a portfolio of losing trades or positions that have yet to start working. Again, that may be fine if you're at a fund that gives you the luxury of being able to have patience and withstand portfolio drawdowns. But, in most shops, it is important to have a mix of trades that are currently working and those that you believe will ultimately work and not experience too much downside. You can quickly dig quite a large hole with a book filled with positions trending against you. A bit of portfolio common sense here.

- **"Please, Just Make It Stop!"** A common tendency with PMs is exiting a poorly performing position at the first instance of a turnaround in the price. With poor trades, PMs can feel that the position is forever doomed. They just want the pain to end, but they also fear selling out at the absolute bottom. As such, there is a strong temptation to free themselves from the trade with any improved performance in the price. However, many times that initial uptick is the beginning of a new positive trend. Thus, one's desire to ease the pain and capitalize on a small improvement in a bad position might prevent them from riding the trade back to much higher levels.

Jay Trotter *(played by Richard Dreyfuss): ..the only reason I won is that you didn't bet! You are the unluckiest person in the world!*
Looney: *Am not!*
Jay Trotter: *Am!*
Looney: *Am not!*
Jay Trotter: *Am! [pulling out his racing form]*
Jay Trotter: *Who do you like in the second?*
Looney: *The six horse looks pretty good….*
Jay Trotter: *[dramatically crosses out the six horse on his racing form] You got a brother?*
Looney: *In Cleveland.*
Jay Trotter: *Call him up, ask him who he likes. I figure it's in the blood!*

Movie: Let It Ride

Chapter 4:

Know Your Horse

I love this brief exchange from 1989 movie "*Let It Ride*" with Richard Dreyfuss. In the movie, Dreyfuss plays the part of Jay Trotter, a down-and-out horserace junkie who surrounds himself with other unfortunate fellow gamblers at the track. The comedy takes place on a day where Trotter suddenly finds himself on a string of very good luck. Rather than analyzing the race sheets and details of each horse, Trotter decides to go with a new strategy of betting on the misfortune of his friends, most notably his best buddy, Looney.

Trotter continues his contrarian tactic throughout the day by going with unloved horses. He wins each race that he bets and then, as the title suggests, "Lets it Ride" on the next race. Energized by this newly-found confidence, he even crosses the main mobster/bookie of the racetrack, Tony Cheesburger (great name!), who mocks Trotter's brief bout of good fortune.

> *"The four horse! Nobody bets the four horse, Trotter. The four horse is a joke. They let little kiddies on the four horse to have their picture taken."*
>
> *Tony Cheesburger, Let It Ride*

In the last race, Trotter takes a thorough survey of the crowd and comes up with a long-shot horse that absolutely no one likes. Of course, the horse wins the race in a photo-finish (pretty predictable in happy-go-lucky films like this) and the crowd goes wild. The movie ends with the crowd cheering to Trotter and his oblivious wife asking, "Why are they cheering?" To which Trotter answers, "Because I'm having a VERY good day."

Unlike the movies, "Let It Ride" bets are generally not a good idea when investing. Nevertheless, I think the film is a fun illustration of the importance of knowing (or in this case, really *not* knowing) what your true bet is. Trotter, probably because of his failed gambling past, decided he would try a tactic of not seeking out any real information or analysis on the horses, and instead employ a strategy of just going against his friends and the crowd. He never really knew what factors he was betting on, what the horse had done in the past, who the jockey was, or why it might be a good day for that horse to win. As such, he was truly flying (or riding) blind and guessing. That's fine on the horse track and for feel-good comedies, but not in the investment world.

Regardless if your investment process leads you to take the favorite horse or the longshot, it is critical that you are keenly aware and in touch with the true bet you are making. **The due diligence of your work should be thorough and follow a set regimen as discussed earlier. But, in the end, it should lead you to one succinct thesis of why you believe the opportunity exists and how you will make money.**

This thesis may relate to something you just discovered or it could be the original idea you had when you started your work. In any case, it should be unambiguous and relatively easy for you to understand and explain. If your idea is overly esoteric, you run the risk that the market will never come around to your line of thinking. Instead, it is important to have a thesis that is relevant to most investors, will be recognized by the Street, and will be consequential to the pricing of the security if you are correct. After all, we aren't doing this for practice. We need to get paid when we are correct.

Some other issues to think about when crafting a thesis are:

- Is the thesis mainly a macro bet, or does it involve an idiosyncratic issue for the company?
- Will I be able to track how my thesis is playing out, or is there a binary event that will decide the fate of my trade?
- If I am right, will I feel lucky? (Being lucky generally is not a good investment objective.)
- How long will it take for my thesis to play out? If it's a long time, is it worth the opportunity cost to my portfolio?

- Could I be too early or too late to the trade?
- How widely-held is my thesis? Is it part of the consensus? (Again, that doesn't mean it is wrong.)
- Am I working with a bias just to confirm my original idea?

The Investment Summary

After you have finished your initial work, you should put together some sort of investment write-up or summary. You should do this regardless if you move forward and initiate the trade or if you decide to pass on it. In cases where I have been lazy and not made the effort of documenting my ideas and work, I have often regretted it. That is especially the case if the position went against me, as I had nothing to fall back on and was left with only my memories of why I liked the idea in the first place. Also, by summarizing the investment, it made me consider more closely if I really believed in what I was writing. Several times, I've decided not to initiate a position after I wrote the summary because it became obvious to me as I wrote it that my reasoning was not very compelling.

I don't believe investment write-ups necessarily have to be very lengthy. Some firms may prefer a detailed written review of each trade. On the other hand, if you have a good format, you may be able to neatly summarize the key points and details on one page. Regardless, there are a few critical elements to any investment presentation.

A well-thought out thesis, or investment overview, is probably on the top of the list. Your thesis doesn't need to be extremely detailed, but should highlight the main factor or elements you believe have created the mispricing. My preference is then to support the thesis with a number of bullet points concerning both company-specific and industry issues.

The write-up should always include a risk section. Don't list the generic risks found in most deal prospectuses, but spell out the specific risks as you see them for the company…the ones that might keep you up at night. Next, I believe investment summaries should outline potential catalysts for the trade and important upcoming events and dates for the company. Finally, in addition to the standard financial figures and trading information, it should include a range of estimates and target prices that represent outcomes for your base case, your best case, and your risk case. For some investments, such as potential take-out targets, you might add a "very best" case. Or, for highly-leveraged or volatile companies, you could add a "risk-risk" case, which would have more downside than your expected risk scenario.

Many PMs and analysts once they have finished their work and initiate the position, then make the mistake of discarding or setting aside the investment summary and not referring to it again. Rather, it is important to keep your investment summary at hand and continue to evaluate and build upon your original work. By doing so, you can frequently review your thoughts and conclusion and determine if they are still valid.

Thesis Creep and Creating an Alternative Thesis

Stale ideas run the risk of "*thesis creep*," which occurs when a position in your portfolio now represents a different bet than your original idea. This can happen when a key catalyst has an unexpected outcome, or if the catalyst comes and goes without a major reaction in the share price. In those cases, it is important to critically reassess the position and determine if your thesis is still sound.

A typical mistake with a position that has not gone your way is to come up with an alternative thesis to take the place of the original thesis. For instance, the original thesis may be that earnings for a particular company will be greater than the Street expects for various reasons. But then, after the company surprises you by falling short of earnings expectations and lowering guidance, you may come up with the alternative reasoning that, with the stock now lower, it is cheap relative to its peers. That may be a fine thesis. But it wasn't the original thesis for the trade. Therefore, you should make a critical assessment if the new thesis is strong enough to justify holding, or even adding to, the position. Also, ask yourself if you are merely looking for reasons not to admit defeat by exiting the position.

Some of my worst trades were positions where my thesis changed from my original idea. In many of those, the trade went from bad to worse, as whatever issue that nullified or disproved my first thesis continued to drive the share price against me. Others investors may have had a similar thesis and were now unwinding their positions, thus adding to the negative price momentum. By looking for a reason to keep the position and not take the loss, I opened myself up for a much larger loss.

My worst experience with this was my long position in Walter Energy, Inc. (NYSE: WLT) in early 2013. Walter is a US and Canadian producer of metallurgical coal, which is used in the production of steel. At the time I initiated the position, met coal prices were on a downtrend after spiking multiple times in prior years. The prior strength in prices mainly related to flooding in Queensland, Australia (a large producing region for met coal) and strong demand from China, which was dramatically growing its steel production and in turn met coal consumption. It was widely believed that the Chinese were the marginal cost producers and that their average breakeven cost was around $140/ton. Therefore, it was thought by many that prices at this level should have some support, as the high-cost Chinese producers would sensibly cut production at lower prices, reducing supply. The idea of price support at $140/ton was given further credence since prices in the prior year had fallen and bounced at approximately this level. As such, my original expectation was that the met coal price would again bottom and bounce near the $140/ton figure, resulting in a large relief rally for Walter.

Unfortunately, when prices hit $140/ton this time, they didn't bounce but fell further to $120/ton by mid-2013 (before going even lower in following years). Reasons for this were (1) continued strong production from industry-leader BHP in Australia, who had low-cost production and unadmittedly was seeking to drive out the high-cost players, particularly in the U.S.; (2) unlike prior years, storm activity did not hinder Australian production; (3) the cost curve for Australian producers shifted down on weakness in the Australian dollar; (4) many of the Chinese met coal producers were State-Owned Enterprises (SEOs), who felt relatively little financial pressure to cut supply at low prices; and (5) new met coal supply was still being added, while demand was beginning to slow from emerging markets, particularly China.

Such low prices were problematic for Walter, who had many high-cost mines and was swimming in debt because of a recent acquisition. So, even with Walter down significantly from where I initially bought the stock, the correct move would have been to unwind the position once I realized the fundamentals had changed where prices were no longer supported at a floor of $140/ton. My thesis was wrong and prices had precipitously dropped well below that level. It should have been time to move on, especially considering the amount of debt Walter was carrying. Instead, I resisted and began to create an alternative thesis on how Walter could survive in a $120/ton environment while waiting for supply to be cut and prices to rally. In hindsight, it is easy to see that I turned to this alternative thesis to justify holding the stock and not lock in the sizeable book loss.

The problem was that the rest of the Street was not so constructive on Walter. Hedge funds correctly sensed blood in the water given the company's large debt load and high costs. In addition to shareholders simultaneously rushing to the exit doors, new funds were adding additional price pressure by shorting the stock. Fortunately, I unwound my position before it got even worse. (Walter filed for bankruptcy in mid-2015.) Still, the large loss stung as it offset many of my favorable trades with positive P&L that year. The experience reminded me that commodity prices can dip well into the cost curve until there is a lagged supply response. Moreover, it reinforced to me the need to be more diligent in questioning my original thesis and not coming up with a secondary thesis to justify holding the position. Cutting the position earlier in the process would have saved a lot of pain in my book at that time.

In general, when your original thesis no longer holds, you must fight the common error of the Endowment Effect and not maintain a predisposition to hang on just because a security is in your portfolio or because the stock is already down considerably. Again, the best practice is to keep your investment summaries at hand and continuously consider if the thesis to your investment is still valid. **If you conclude your thesis is stale or now irrelevant, you should be biased to unwinding the trade rather than coming up with an alternative reason to hold on to it.**

Focus on the Idiosyncratic over the Macro

Most sell-side institutional investor conferences offer clients one-on-one meetings with the management teams presenting at the conference. Unfortunately, in almost all cases, investors far outnumber the companies at the conferences, particularly for corporations where meetings are in high demand. Therefore, only the largest clients actually get true one-on-ones. The other meetings are really small group gatherings with management. I'm typically fine with that, particularly as it allows me to hear the thoughts and questions of some of my peers. However, I admit that I get frustrated when a fellow institutional investor obviously hasn't done their homework on a company and asks a generic, pointless question, thus wasting our limited time with management.

A good example comes from a small group meeting I attended a few years ago at the Bank of Montreal's (BMO) premier annual global metals and mining conference in Florida. The conference is undoubtedly the most popular event in the sector and allows for an investor to meet with a plethora of companies over the three-day duration. To facilitate this, BMO establishes fairly brief 30-minute time slots for each one-on-one session or small group meeting, and then rigidly enforces the time limit with a digital clock in each meeting room that counts down from 30 minutes. It's a lot like speed dating and doesn't leave much time for chit-chat. To get the most out of the meetings, the intention is for investors to have their key questions ready. This is especially important in small group meetings, where investors must take turns asking their questions, and therefore typically do not want to waste their turn by inquiring about a trivial matter or an issue where management's response would be obvious.

In this particular small group meeting I attended with a gold producer, an unprepared investor asked, "So, are you bullish on the gold price?" A few of us in the meeting immediately gazed at him with disdain. Really? This guy had one opportunity for a question and that's it?!! I wanted to interject, "Of course, they are bullish on gold. They are a gold company! Moreover, they have no more clue about the direction of the gold price than you or me ...AND, by the way, your worthless question is probably going to take five minutes off our precious clock, as management gives us their incredibly biased view of gold!"

The reality is that contemplating, debating, and obsessing over largely macro-driven issues, like the gold price, is often a waste of time. It's generally very difficult to gain any real edge or attain any key information or perspective not already possessed by multitudes of other investors. Of course, basing your investment thesis on solely macro issues can be profitable, but it doesn't typically give you an advantage over the investing masses. A better route, in my view, is focusing on the company- or industry-specific fundamentals, where you may actually attain some sort of edge to those who have not done the fundamental research. With such positions, it's typically easier to gain conviction and possibly not have to change your view because of external events that are uncontrollable by the company. **A devoted, research-driven effort to uncover the mispriced, idiosyncratic issues with a company is at most times far superior to a thesis formed only through macro variables.**

Your Thesis Should Not Hinge on Getting Lucky

When I was a growing up, I probably watched the wrestling movie Vision Quest a hundred times. The film had a fairly similar storyline to many other 1980s flicks (e.g., Rocky, Karate Kid, Hoosiers), where the underdog devotedly trains, overcomes all odds, and in the end defeats the dramatically-favored Goliath of the movie. In this case, Louden Swain (played by Mathew Modine) serves as the underdog, a relatively inexperienced wrestler who drops two weight classes to take on an unbeaten, three-time state champion and beast of a competitor, Brian Shute. The lead-up to the ending match features Swain's dedicated efforts to make the lower weight, Shute's herculean training measures (including walking up stadium stairs with a log on his back), and a love story accompanied in the background by several Madonna and Journey classics. What a great movie!

In the culmination of the film, Swain is trailing late in the match when he catches Shute in a spectacular over-under hip toss and pins him on his back for the victory. And the crowd goes wild…of course. Who in the movie theater didn't predict that? It's also pretty obvious the film writers were not going to have Swain win by narrowly outscoring Shute, just like Rocky wasn't going to beat Ivan Drago by a split decision. A last-minute, dramatic victory naturally makes for a much better movie and is consistent with the positive themes with these type of films where "anything is possible" and "never count yourself out." It works particularly well with sports like wrestling and boxing, where the underdog can be losing decisively, but suddenly win the contest by catching their opponent with one critical move or punch.

But even with that possibility, I wonder what the pre-match odds would have been in Las Vegas with the Swain vs Shute match. Undoubtedly, the odds would have reflected what was obvious to myself and most wrestlers who watched the movie. That is Shute would have crushed Swain essentially every time. It's simple. Undefeated, three-time state champions just don't lose to inexperienced wrestlers, especially when the other wrestler is weak from cutting weight. Sure, like the scenario in the movie, there was a faint chance that Swain could have won the match with a fluky, timely move. However, betting beforehand on him getting lucky by such an occurrence would have seemed extremely irrational….just like Jay Trotter "letting it ride" on the 50-to-1 horse would have made little sense.

In investing, getting lucky can occur in numerous ways, through a corporate takeout, a project win, a breakthrough discovery, or many other fortunate happenings. The possibilities of such an occurrence can make an investment seem very attractive. Nevertheless, when analyzing a trade, one must critically assess the likelihood and their conviction of the occurrence actually coming true. Often, the potential event represents merely hope in the eyes of investors, or at best an outside potential that cannot be quantified. In those cases, the main thesis of the trade probably should not rest on that possibility. Instead, your thesis should be one where the odds seem stacked in your favor and where attaining your targeted return on the investment will not be determined by things working out just perfectly or a largely improbable event taking place. **In your mind, the correction of the mispricing in the market should be mostly likely solved by the fundamentally-derived crux of your thesis, not by an out-of-the-blue development.**

Of course, I'm not saying the potential for your investment to benefit from an unpredictable event is not desirable, especially if it represents to some degree a call option that you believe is not factored into the price of the security. However, those opportunities should typically be viewed as gravy on top of your core thesis for the investment and should not be relied upon if your core thesis becomes invalid. For instance, if your main thesis of earnings estimates for a company being too low fails, you probably should not rely on your view that the company is a possible takeout candidate to save your trade. Again, you must resist betting on Hail Mary's and focus on playing the probabilities of what will give you the greatest chance of success.

Going Back to Prior Positions

One way to be in touch with the core bet you are making is by going back to successful trades you have made in the past. By doing so, you can utilize the knowledge and understanding you have retained from your experiences, as well as build upon prior notes, financial models, presentations, etc. I feel that by revisiting past positions, I often have more conviction in those ideas because of my previous experiences. I am also typically able to shorten my due diligence time, as I benefit from my prior work and thoughts rather than starting from scratch.

Still, it is important not to merely rely on your prior knowledge with such positions by being complacent and cutting corners when updating your research. Companies change, as does the environment affecting them. You shouldn't assume that just because the price of a security is back to the level where you previously initiated a position that it now represents the same bet as before. Once you've revisited the idea and are again up to speed on the issues, you may realize there are now greater risks with the position or that this time you should be patient and wait for more attractive set-up levels.

I learned this lesson the hard way on a couple occasions, most notably involving one of my favorite recurring trades: a pair trade of Flour Inc. (NYSE: FLR) and Jacobs Engineering (NYSE: JEC). The companies are two of the largest US-based engineering and construction firms and are both well-respected and generally well-run corporations. There are various differences between the two (e.g., Flour has more of an international presence, while more of Jacob's jobs are domestic). Still, they are similar enough that they have tended to trade largely in tandem. Over the course of their histories, when one stock has meaningfully outperformed the other, the performance gap is corrected in a reasonable period. The mean-reverting quality of this pair has made it a frequent position in my portfolio. At times, I have almost instinctively put on the trade when the performance gap reached a level where I had previously initiated a position. However, the times when I ran into trouble were when I relied too heavily on my prior experiences and did not fully account for changes that had occurred with the two companies or the current industry environment. In those cases, the performance gap tended to blow-out well beyond the recent ranges and led to some unpleasant initial book losses. This was while I belatedly and frantically researched what had changed and hoped the mean-reversion tendency of the trade would take hold again.

It all goes back to understanding the true bet you are making and having a prudent thesis upon which you can judge your position. Again, the best practice is to diligently form a sound thesis, document your work, constantly update your research, and persistently evaluate if your thesis still holds. Maintaining the discipline to perform these necessary steps can be time consuming and isn't always easy, but I believe it is a critical process to successful investing.

"I've been thinking about this, Mr. Hand. If I'm here and you're here, doesn't that make it our time?"

Jeff Spicoli, Movie: Fast Times at Ridgemont High

Chapter 5:

It's All About Timing

When I was growing up, my father was President of the local bank in our small town. Anyone who knows my dad knows that he has quite a personality and is generally not short on conversation. And when he wasn't chatting about banking matters, Oklahoma football, or a putt he almost made, he was often talking about my wrestling. A frequent party in his discussions was a former renowned Blackwell wrestling coach and NCAA champion, the late Chuck Hetrick. (I'm violating my "no names" policy on this one to recognize what was the greatness and genuine character of this man.) The two would often start talking about a particular match and ultimately end up on the floor of my father's office with Coach Hetrick showing my dad a move that I should incorporate in my wrestling. That was all fine until a bank customer would show up and see the two grown men rolling on the floor together. Unfortunately, this poorly-timed occurrence happened on multiple occasions. So, before word got around town (which doesn't take long!), my father and Coach decided maybe it was best to demonstrate moves when I was around and on a wrestling mat away from the bank.

Timing is everything. In investing, understanding the correct time to initiate a trade and when to size up or down or exit is key. In many cases, it's equally as important as the trade itself. "I've never been wrong, just too early or too late" is an old investment joke. But, in actuality, being too early or too late is often the equivalent of being wrong. Very few funds can lose money being wrong for an extended period of time and still honestly say their investments are on course or, more importantly, convince their investors that their plan is still on track. Moreover, I would argue those that can wait years on years for their thesis to play out really have the luxury of not having to be right at all. In many cases, their 12- or 24-month price objective becomes a rolling target, resulting in an investment that is always on the come.

Have a Targeted Time Horizon

The inability to have a ballpark guess of when you will make money on an idea often really nullifies the trade altogether and unfortunately can make the idea rather useless. In some ways, I have viewed bearish bets on China in this vein. Just prior to my first visit to China in May 2011, the country's economy appeared to be bouncing back strongly after the recent global financial crisis. This was highlighted by dramatic growth in fixed asset investment that was largely thanks to the government's massive stimulus program put in place during the recent global financial downturn. Nevertheless, at that time, there were already worrisome stories about ghost cities, the shadow lending market, and unsustainable debt formation. As a result, I was told by my boss to "look for cracks in the story" that were not apparent in the overall government reported figures.

During the small group tour, I was amazed by the sheer scope of the country and the tremendous level of construction activity that seemed to back up the reports. This was particularly evident in Tier 2 and Tier 3 cities we visited like Shenyang, Anshan, and Nanning, which by population would be Tier 1 cities almost anywhere else. Essentially everywhere I looked, cranes and construction projects filled my view. The closest comparison I had previously was a 2006 property tour I took of Miami. But the level of construction I saw in China extraordinarily dwarfed that. Some noteworthy memories from the trip included driving by a newly-built major athletic complex in a Tier 3 city that looked like a football stadium for a decent size US college, only to realize there were two replicas right behind it. I guess those were for the times when the city needed to hold massively-attended events simultaneously. Also, I won't forget flying into the fairly small Nanning airport at night and driving into what we thought would be a quaint little town, only to feel like we were suddenly in the middle of Las Vegas. It seemed like they had built all of this without telling anyone.

While I was amazed by the extent of the construction occurring, the analytical side of me naturally got very bearish. I remembered how the Miami market fared after my tour once the US property market crashed, and suddenly those cracks in the story I was supposed to be looking for seemed like gaping holes.

Still, as I learned more about the command economy of China and attained a better appreciation for the long-term demographic drivers in place, it became apparent to me that the party was far from over. The government was highly incentivized to keep growth high, primarily by boosting government-funded construction levels. This large fixed asset investment prepared the country for further urbanization, where over 10 million people are leaving the countryside and entering cities each year. It also kept job growth high, and thus ensured that people were busy and happy (i.e., not protesting the government). Moreover, by encouraging new production, or even overcapacity in many sectors, China moves forward toward its objective to become more self-sufficient and better prepared for eventually a greater consumer-driven economy. In many cases, it has become clear the country is more concerned about having not enough capacity than having overcapacity. In emphasizing the need to prepare, the Chinese point to their highway system, which twenty years ago was largely empty but now is packed with traffic.

I visited China again in 2014, touring cities in the Shandong Providence like Jinan, Zibo, and Rizhao. During my group's visit to the countryside, we saw what I had seen three years previously, a massive number of developments under construction among Tier 2-4 cities and literally new cities being created from villages on the outskirts of existing cities. In each city we passed, I was again busily taking pictures of the rows and rows of Monopoly-like buildings and cranes that littered the skyline.

Similar to my prior visit, it was difficult not to have a bearish outlook to what appeared to be dramatic overbuilding, but this time at a later stage. However, with this trip, I had a better grasp on the importance of timing. Even if I was on the right track, my bearish stance from three years prior certainly had not played out. Rather, the government had continued to push investment growth, favoring that over reforms and debt controls. Therefore, even with other pressing reform issues like corruption and pollution on the government's plate, I was wary of being overly cautious, as I had grown an appreciation for China's ability to stay on the growth treadmill for an uncertain period.

Over the past couple years, the bearish China thesis has played out to a much larger degree. The inevitable slowdown in growth (partly due to the law of big numbers), impact of new reforms, continued high debt formation, and volatility in the local stock market has concerned both local and global investors. The result has been big hits to commodity prices and to international companies with high exposure to the country. The longer-term demographic trends, such as urbanization and the upgrading of the Chinese consumer, seem to remain in place. However, there are now many more questions on government controls, the rate of growth, and how China transitions away from construction-driven expansion to consumption-driven growth.

I find the issues surrounding China immensely interesting and greatly important to global investing. However, my point with this is not to detail the bull and bear cases for the country, which could fill many more pages and still only scratch the surface of the topic. Instead, my focus here is just to empathize what I have largely viewed as the futility of trying to predict the timing of China's demise. The government's ability to dictate growth and its post-crisis policies supporting expansion has made calling the exact turning point for China very difficult, even despite increasing evidence bolstering the case for more difficult times ahead.

I recently read a story about a large hedge fund that was very bearish on China on the thesis that the country is adding credit faster than its growth rate. That's a great reason to be bearish. And, in recent quarters, that view seems to be playing out. However, the article stated that this fund has had that bet for five years. I wonder if their investment time horizon was that long when they initiated the trade. In many camps, five years is the same as being wrong, even if you're on the verge of being correct.

Exhibit 11: Notable Quotes from My Visit to China, May 2014:

Visitor on tour: *"Is it supposed to rain or is that pollution?"*

Iron Ore trader: *"I buy iron ore. When I think it's about to go higher, I buy more. When I am wrong, I start to hedge. I don't know..I just guess."*

Power plant manager: *"White smoke means desulfurization is on. Yellow smoke means not on. At night, you do not see color of smoke."*

Tour Host: *"Don't worry there are no guns in China, just knives"* – said after our bus driver jumped out of the bus in Zibo and punched another driver in his truck for cutting him off.

Granted, I don't know at what point an investment goes from being classified as "patient" to being just wrong. I suspect that depends mainly on the attitude of your investors. Still, having at least a general idea of the time horizon of your investment is paramount. **Investments made with a good thesis, but no idea of when that thesis may play out, simply are not very good investments in my view.**

Respect Momentum

Earlier we discussed contrarian investing and betting against the crowd, which can be a very profitable strategy if you maintain the right mindset. After recognizing the opportunity to take an unpopular position, the next key aspect of the investment is timing the initial trade and building up the position size. While ultimately your entry level may prove attractive, no one wants to step in front of a locomotive and start a position with a nice book loss from which to dig out. Instead, easing into a trade or waiting until momentum slows is generally more desirable.

Respecting momentum is immensely important when deciding the best time to invest. I've learned this the hard way on several occasions, particularly as it relates to commodities, which can trend in one direction for a surprisingly long time. The aforementioned book "*Reminiscences of a Stock Operator*" discusses the concept of the "path of least resistance," which securities tend to follow in the short term.[1] This concept goes hand in hand with the laws of physics, or more precisely Newton's First Law of Motion, which states "an object at rest stays at rest and an object in motion stays in motion with the same speed and in the same direction unless acted upon by an unbalanced force."[2]

Relating to the investing world, a stock that is falling on negative sentiment or a reaction to an earnings report continues to fall until supported by a counter force (e.g., value buying, short covering, market news, etc.). Thus, in the absence of those counter forces, a security can continue along its path of least resistance well beyond what you may think is appropriate. It took me many poorly-timed trades to appreciate this. But eventually, I learned not to trade just on my impulse reaction that a stock's move seems ridiculous or overdone. On many of those occasions, the stock's move became even more overdone in the short term and offered an even better entry point once the momentum subsided.

In my job as a hedge fund PM, I once had a new boss whose background was primarily with lower-beta stocks and was unfamiliar with the volatility and momentum of commodity-related stocks that comprised much of my coverage universe. I was having a bout of misfortune in the markets when he called me and asked, "What's hurting your book today?" I explained it was mainly one position that was again down a large percentage. He then looked at how many standard deviations the position had moved against me in the past week and, without listening much to the reason for the move, said that I should add to the trade. It made sense to do so statistically and especially since I believed my thesis was still intact. So I added. However, the next day the position fell hard again, and he called and asked, "So what's the problem today?" I answered, "Remember that trade we added to yesterday? Well, it hurts even more today."

Please note I am not advocating being swept up by market opinions or not capitalizing when the market presents you an opportunity to increase your bet at a large discount. I'm merely saying one should respect the trend before being so eager to oppose momentum. Building up the size of a trade too quickly in the midst of strongly opposing momentum is an excellent way to generate a quick large book loss. And, depending on the size of the loss, you may be forced out of the position before it reverses direction and allows you to make your money back.

At the same time, it is important to remember the old market truism that "they don't ring a bell at the bottom." As such, a profitable strategy can be to establish price points at which to gradually build up a position. For a stock that was at $100 per share and now is at $85 and trending down, you might initiate a 25-50% position now and then set targets to add at $80 and $75. Thus, you've at least somewhat capitalized on the 15% downward move if the stock rebounds back to $100. You will also establish a lower average entry price and a lower initial book loss if the security continues to trend lower. This practice can take some of the sting out of opposing momentum.

OK, what about playing *with* the momentum then? In other words, betting with a trend that is already in place. Naturally, to make money, one doesn't need to bottom-tick the price of a security or necessarily get in during the first part of the trade. Playing the last 50% of a stock's move is just as profitable as playing the first 50%. Personally, in cases where I have engaged in buying a momentum stock, or "trend following," I have never been able to convince myself to buy the stock at its absolute high.

Rather, I like to initiate a position when the security is down a standard deviation or so from its price trendline, but is still distinctly on an upwards trajectory. In other words, I look for kinks, or "buying opportunities" (ugh, I said it again), in the upward-trending charts.

Once a trend-following position is in place, I try to be disciplined to unwind the trade (or at least much of it) at my target price and not just hold the position until it begins to fail, a common mistake among momentum players. To guard against the trade turning course before it reaches my target, I have often put in place a rolling stop-loss. The stop-losses I've set are typically 4-8% below the high in the stock in the time that I owned the position, depending on the volatility of the stock. That means that if I bought a momentum stock below its trendline, I would normally unwind the trade on further weakness rather than adding to it. This is a different strategy than for a value stock that has underperformed, where the risk-reward tradeoff seems to have improved on further weakness. For a stock with momentum (typically at the top right corner of the price chart), the risk-reward is generally skewed to the downside once the momentum stalls. As such, establishing a rolling stop-loss prevents a potential outsized loss if a stock pulls back to substantially lower levels.

The following chart shows an example of a rolling stop-loss set at 7% below the prior high in the stock (since the entry point). In the example, you may have opportunistically bought the stock at $26 below its trendline, with the stock then rebounding to $34. With the rolling stop-loss, the stop-loss is then triggered after the stock falls below $31.62 (7% below the prior high of $34). Of course, in perfect hindsight, you wish you would had sold at $34. But, once the momentum breaks, the rolling-stop allows you to maintain a profit in the trade (making the term "stop-*loss*" actually a misnomer) and prevents you from riding the stock way back to your entry point or below.

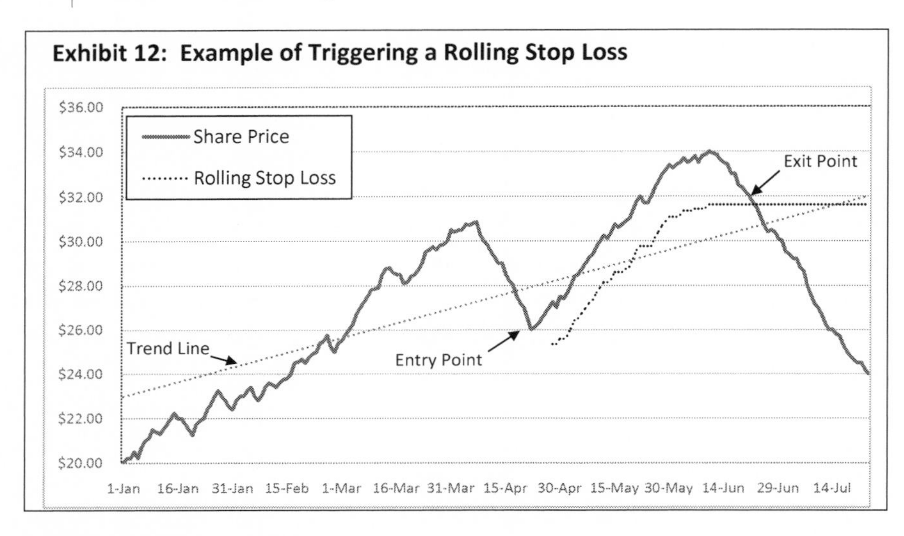

Exhibit 12: Example of Triggering a Rolling Stop Loss

Don't Wait for the Perfect Trades

So when are optimal times to initiate a trade, or to unwind a position? I don't think there are simple answers here. For one, I don't believe you should wait and swing at only perfect pitches. Sure, your goal should be to find those ideal opportunities where everything seems to have lined up in your favor and the risks appear remote. But, if you're honest with yourself, you will recognize those opportunities don't come around with great frequency. In fact, I tend to uncover one or two such trades a year, if any at all. Waiting to play only those opportunities where everything has lined up perfectly will likely result in having not much money invested or a very concentrated portfolio. Conversely, most trades have a very realistic risk case and an issue that even may keep you up at night. That doesn't mean they are not good ideas. The risk-reward tradeoff may still be dramatically in your favor, strongly presenting the case for inclusion in your portfolio.

It's also important to realize that just because you have finished your due diligence, and now better understand the opportunity, does not mean that it's the right time to initiate the trade. You may have just attained a clear understanding of a company or learned of an important piece of information, but that issue may be well understood by other investors and already discounted in the stock price. Alternatively, you may be too early to the idea. An important catalyst may be months away, or it may simply take some time before Old Man Market gives credit to your line of thinking. Although you may choose not to initiate a position immediately after you've finished your work, that doesn't mean your work is in vein. Instead, you should keep your research at hand and up-to-date and then look for better pricing opportunities so that you will ultimately get paid for your efforts.

Catalysts are important. As discussed previously, you should search for key events that will serve as inflection points for your trade. It's vital to regularly evaluate the quality of your catalyst, as well as your conviction in it. Also, continue to think about the potential for it to have a meaningful impact on the security or to change sentiment, as well as the extent the catalyst is known among market participants. Finally, consider if the potential upside from the catalyst is worth the event risk if it does not play out as you expect.

Know When Not to Play

Holding a full position into an event risk is fine if you have some level of conviction on the outcome and the potential price reaction to the event. However, with much of the price action in today's market environment decided by short-term players and their positioning, it's often difficult or impossible to know how a security will react to a given piece of news. Thanks to crowdedness on one side of the trade, stocks frequently move in illogical directions and in greater magnitudes than a prudent investor would expect.

One can talk themselves in circles pondering the potential price action following many events. For instance, when thinking about the possible reaction to a company's upcoming earnings release, I've had conversations with my team that go something like this:

> *"Well, we want to be long going into the event because we think earnings will be good."*
>
> *"Yeah, but everyone knows that. It's in the stock already. It's probably better to be short actually."*
>
> *"True. But, we can't be short. Look at short interest levels. Everyone's short. So we should be long."*
>
> *"Yes, long for sure. But what if management updates guidance? We know estimates are too high. The stock should trade lower on that."*
>
> *"But isn't the market aware that management is conservative? Remember when the stock traded higher on lower guidance three quarters ago?"*

> *"OK, let me get this straight. Our fundamental analysis says we want to be long. But our investor analysis says we want to be short...but possibly long...but then again maybe short because guidance...or long. What derivative are we on now? Does anyone have a coin to flip?"*

What a pointless conversation. We call this kind of deliberation "Princess Bride analysis," based on a humorous scene from that classic movie. (In the scene, two characters engage in a battle of wits, where one must choose to drink from the cup not containing poisonous iocane powder. Vizzini, the villain, gives an illogical, round-about speech, changing his decision several times before making his selection. I recommend Youtubing the scene if you haven't watched the movie. It's sadly a terrific analogy to some of the pointless deliberations that take place in investing.)

In our example, our fundamental analysis on the quarterly results may be correct, but it's obvious that we have no idea how the stock will react. In those cases where you really have no clue on the potential price outcome, it may be better just not to play or at least to reduce your exposure into the event risk.

The futility of Princess Bride-like analysis can at times also be observed with individuals attempting to outwit the broader market. Here's a good recent example: The financial media unleashes fear-mongering commentary that the Federal Reserve is soon to raise interest rates and that will be bad for the market. But, it appears during the weeks going into the Fed announcement that expectation has become commonplace. So the press speculates that the market is going up because investors are comfortable with the anticipated rate increase, and now we just need to get it over. However, closer to the event, they comment that the market has already priced in that comfort, and so there is now risk to a "sell-the-event" decline in stock prices. BUT, the "sell-the-event" weakness actually occurs *before* the event. So with the market down, the pundits are back to saying we need to buy stocks on the news again. Unfortunately, any investors following this absurd back and forth are likely fairly confused by now and may also be looking for a coin to flip.

The reality is reacting to the news might be a good course of action for a couple hours after the Fed release, but then, as often the case, the market may swing hard in the opposite direction (whatever direction that is) not long after the initial reaction. This gives financial market commentators the opportunity to come up with a reason for that move as well. All of this is even more ludicrous if you observe some traders on interest rate or currency exchange desks who, when new economic data is released, pound their key boards trading in one direction after someone on their trading floor yells "good number!"...then only to pound their key boards trading in the opposite direction moments later. Seriously? What's the point of all this? Does anyone really have any edge? Or does everyone just feel the need to do something that seems important in reaction to a big financial event? I can imagine Old Man Market chuckling at the ridiculousness of it all.

Don't Chase

My father likes to tell a story about his roommate in the early 1960s when he was stationed in San Diego with the Navy, a fellow enlistee named Pete Smith (or something close to that). Evidentially, Pete was a financially opportunistic guy and in an effort to scrounge up some money, he once submitted a small classified ad in the local paper simply stating, "This is your last chance to give Pete Smith $5. Please send to ....." My father says he was astounded when shortly afterwards his friend received numerous letters containing $5 bills.

This story reminds me of a frequent investing mistake of chasing stocks after a large move. Similar to responding to the ad in the newspaper, investors often get coaxed into thinking they will never get the chance again to purchase a stock at its former price. On the long side, too often investors get caught up in the hype of the day and convince themselves that the price is only going up from here, and that they might as well get in now or miss out completely. However, in most cases, buying a security immediately after a large, reactionary spike isn't a prudent move. Yes, the bounce might be well justified, but whatever has caused it has obviously become well-known at that time. And, while you may think the reason for the bounce could lead to even further gains, the new information is undoubtedly in large part already reflected in the stock price. The mispricing has been recognized by the market and now may even be possibly *overly*-discounted in the stock price.

In most cases, stocks don't move in a linear fashion. Although the new information may continue to drive the stock higher over time, securities in the short-term often experience some level of profit-taking after a large move. Alternatively, other factors (e.g., broader market movements) may push the stock back down to prior levels. So, my advice is to contain your exuberance, don't beat yourself up for missing the move, and wait for another day and a better price.

Exiting the Position

Just as important as selecting the appropriate time to initiate a trade is determining the right time to exit a position. I believe in remaining disciplined on unwinding much, if not all, of a position when it hits your target price. Nevertheless, if you do that, you must also remain disciplined on cutting your losses on some poor performing positions. Otherwise, you risk making a common mistake at all levels of investing of holding your losers too long and selling your winners too quickly. Such behavior goes along with our primal nature of doing what feels good to us. It feels good to recognize a gain in a stock and it feels terrible to record a loss or to see what was once a gain in the books turn into a loss.

The behavioral finance term here is call "*Loss Aversion*." That is that people dislike losing more than they like winning...by a ratio of up to 2:1 based on some studies.[3] Accordingly, investors are risk takers in order to avoid a loss, but are risk-adverse in the face of gains. For instance, Loss Aversion argues that if you told a group of people they could have $3,000 now or take a chance to *win* $10,000 and told a separate, equally-sized group they must *pay* $3,000 or take the same chance where they might *lose* $10,000, more participants in the first group would take the guaranteed money compared to the number of people that would pay $3,000 to avoid the possible loss. Even with the same odds, the thought of losing $10,000 has greater significance to most people than the possibility of winning $10,000. Hence, they are willing to go to greater ends to avoid the loss. On the other hand, taking the easy money seems like the more sensible choice.

Loss Aversion is evident in other areas of our world as well. A University of Pennsylvania Wharton Business School study published in 2011 analyzed the putting of PGA golfers. They found that the professionals were more accurate (i.e., more focused) when putting for a par or bogey than they were if putting for a birdie or eagle. When putting for a par or bogey the golfer is seeking to avoid a poor score on the hole relative to par. Conversely, a birdie or eagle would result in a favorable score relative to par. Even though the overall score is what matters, posting a positive or negative score relative to par on each hole seemed to have a different behavioral impact on the golfers.[4]

Frequently with a losing position, investors fall prey to anther irrational investing strategy called "*Anchoring*." That is the tendency to judge each investment relative to some reference point, such as a prior high in the stock or where you made your initial investment.[5]

Anchoring tends to go hand in hand with a "*Breakeven Strategy*," where investors often hold on to a losing position for the hope that they will just get back to breakeven on the trade.[6] Unfortunately, for positions that have fallen by a large amount, the math to get back to breakeven is not in the investor's favor. For instance, it's no secret that a stock that has fallen by 50% has to double in price to get back to its original level. Many investors fail to recognize the simple mathematics required for a breakeven strategy to be successful.

Loss Aversion and Breakeven Strategy are two behavior pitfalls that prevent investors from making the logical decision to simply take their lumps and punt a losing position. Sustaining outsized losses with such positions, while selling winning positions at more modest price changes, puts the portfolio in a very difficult position and normally yields lackluster returns.

Batting Average and Slugging

At a basic level, portfolio returns are generated by two factors termed by baseball: batting average and slugging. Batting average is simply the percent of your positions that make money, while slugging represents your average gain in a profitable position relative to your average loss in a losing position (simply expressed by your average dollar gain divided by your average dollar loss). A slugging ratio above 1.0 therefore means that you make more on your winners on average than you lose with your unprofitable positions. Similarly, a ratio below 1.0 means that your losing positions are costing you more than you are making with your winners. Thus, the tendency of selling your winners too early and holding on to your losers typically results in a poor slugging ratio. Sticking with the baseball analogy, you are essentially giving up homeruns and hitting singles and doubles. Of course, if you do that on a consistent basis, you must necessarily have a very high batting average to generate positive returns.

The Luck of Having Bad Luck

Finally, as it relates to timing, there is the possibility of just bad luck. Many years ago, a friend and former fellow associate analyst had just taken a new job at a sell-side firm, which was a promotion to a Sr. Research Analyst. He prepared for his initiation of coverage for months. He started by initiating on the stock of Rent-A-Center (NASDAQ: RCII), a company he knew well from researching it as an associate and now as a lead analyst. At the morning research meeting on the day of his initiation (with a "Buy" rating), he walked the institutional equity salesforce through his bullish case and key catalysts for the stock, one being his expectation for positive results in the upcoming quarter. He then asked for questions. Unfortunately, the first person to raise their hand did not have a question, but a statement that Rent-A-Center was on the tape announcing a shortfall in next quarter's earnings. Oops. I don't think my friend had prepared for that one.

Bad luck and bad timing just happen. If you play the game long enough, it's inevitable some of your trades or recommendations will be hit by out-of-the-blue events. Merger and acquisition (M&A) activity is a great example. Sometimes takeouts work in your favor (such as when a company you're long is being purchased by another company) and sometime they work against you (e.g., in a pair position, when a company you are long bids for a company that you are short, which unfortunately can lead to a double whammy of large losses on each side of the trade). In these cases of bad luck, there is really no use of analyzing what went wrong or stewing over the loss. It's generally better just to take the licking and move on.

Exhibit 13: Key points to Timing

1) Have a general idea of the time horizons with your positions.
2) Respect momentum, especially when deciding the timing to initiate a position.
3) Think about lagging into an initial position when a security has strong opposing momentum.
4) Evaluate the quality and potential impact of your catalyst(s).
5) Don't wait for perfect trades. Even good trades have reasonable risk factors.
6) Know when not to play.
7) Don't chase stocks after large, reactionary moves.
8) When determining when to exit a trade, beware of common behavior pitfalls such as loss aversion and breakeven strategy.
9) Consider the two elements that drive a portfolio's return: batting average and slugging.
10) Don't stew over bad luck.

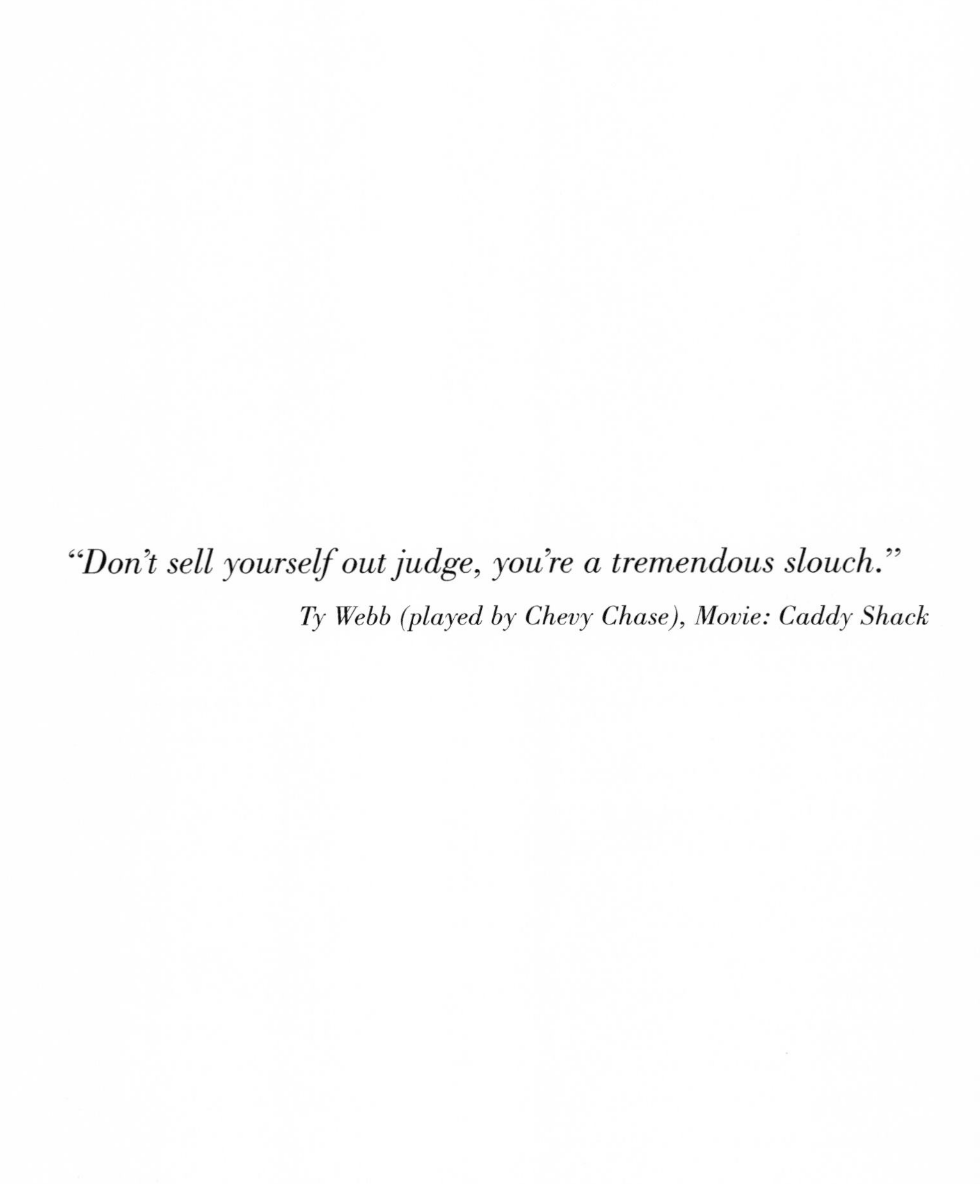

"Don't sell yourself out judge, you're a tremendous slouch."

Ty Webb (played by Chevy Chase), Movie: Caddy Shack

Chapter 6:

Are You Really Sure About This?

During my senior season at Cornell, we wrestled in a dual meet against powerhouse Minnesota. At my weight class, Minnesota had the number one-ranked wrestler in the country. That normally would seem rather daunting (and it did to some degree). However, I had wrestled the same guy during my junior season and lost by a respectable score of 5 to 2. Thus, my hope was that even though this guy was now ranked as the best in the country, I would be able to hang close with him once again. I was typically a pretty good first period wrestler (admittedly less so in the often most important third period). So, not long into the match, I was able to score a fairly quick takedown on the edge of the mat. I was feeling pretty good at that point with my team cheering me on and reinforcing my hope that I could again make this a close match or even somehow win this time.

Then, while coming back to the center of the mat, my opponent gave to his coaches in his corner a look that I'll never forget. It was a simple, yet confident smirk. I did not view it as arrogant, cocky, or disrespectful. Rather, it seemed to simply portray a very high level confidence in himself and conviction that he would ultimately be the victor. It's a bit hard to describe out of the moment. But to me, it was a strong signal to his coaches and team, "Relax, I've got this."

Unfortunately for me, he was correct and the rest of the match was quite lopsided in his favor. Some may say I let him get into my head and that if I had displayed similar confidence, the result could have been different. That's possibly true and maybe I would have been mentally stronger at that moment if I was the wrestler ranked number one in the country. In any case, the match was a good lesson for me, as I later thought about my opponent's confidence and his lack of panic at that time. How could I attain such confidence?...not just in wrestling, but in all that I do.

Just as with sports, having confidence is vital in investing. In order not to be shaken from your ideas, you must have confidence in your abilities and conviction in your work. Otherwise, you become just another one of the sheep ready for the slaughter when Old Man Market turns against you (note I said *when*, not *if*). Having such conviction I believe is the only way to escape the common behavior pitfalls of investing we discussed previously.

But that's easily said when you're not in the pressure of the moment. Unfortunately, it's not as simple when things are not going your way and when it feels like the entire market is against you. **Even the most confident PMs and analysts can be shaken at times. The stress and anxiety presented with each difficult situation is not to be discounted or taken lightly**.

Many years ago, a fellow PM and friend of mine was suffering from a difficult run in his portfolio. He was a seasoned investor, but like many PMs, he was having trouble finding the confidence to fall back on during this difficult time. After another rough day in the market, he was scheduled to interview a local business school student for a potential internship with him the coming summer. After reviewing the candidate's impressive experience and high standardized test scores, he began to feel a bit inferior mentally to the guy, despite the candidate being nearly twenty years his junior. So, after running out of questions, he finally asked him, "How do you feel about working for someone who's not as smart as you?" Classic. I don't think they prepare you for that one in practice interviews in business school. Afterwards, I gave my friend a bit of a hard time when he told me what he had asked. "Come on, man. Who cares about his GMAT score? Think about your experience and the knowledge you've attained all these years of investing. Take pride and confidence in that. He's not nearly as smart as you when it comes to this business or this job. And don't let him think that he is."

I don't mean to belittle my friend here with this funny story. If you play the game long enough, it's inevitable to have periods of self-doubt. I've had plenty over the years. But how do you get out of a rut? **How do you pull yourself out of the downward spiral when it seems that nothing is going your way?**

One way is to look for small victories that can serve as confidence builders and maybe even turning points to reverse your negative momentum. I'm often amazed in sports how one play or one small action by a competitor can totally reverse the tide of a game. Be it from a fumble recovery, a long putt, a three-point shot, or a third period takedown, what was just a hopeless situation can be turned around in seconds. Similarly, in investing, instances like a positive development with a troubled company or the first profitable day for your portfolio after a rough drawdown can be thought of as small victories, which can provide a needed boost to your confidence and outlook. Just as with sports, it's often a mental game we are playing. One day, the market or your portfolio makes no sense and seems like total chaos. Then, the next day you suddenly feel that your stock screen is like the Matrix (from the popular Keanu Reeve's sci-fi movies), where all the pieces logically fit and the opportunities are crystal clear. The key is to build upon small victories and chart a new positive course.

A Balance: Underconfidence vs Overconfidence

Personalities differ, and converse to the prior discussion, many people in the investment industry seem to have no problem with having confidence, even in times when they would do well to have a bit of humility. Many of them suffer from the aforementioned common investing faux pas of overconfidence or Illusory Superiority.

So what's the correct level of confidence one should possess and act upon? Obviously, you don't want to doubt your abilities or ideas and to be shaken by every price move not in your favor. But, you also don't want to fall into the overconfidence trap.

It's a tricky issue and a delicate balance. **Investors must somehow keep in mind that they are generally not as bad as they may think they are when they are doing poorly and not as good as they may think they are when they are hitting it out of the park.** The reality is normally somewhere in the middle. Recognizing such promotes both the required assertive demeanor for the job, but also the humility to respect the market and opposing viewpoints. **In our daily wrestling with Old Man Market, we must maintain a certain level of reverence for our opponent, but still demonstrate a high level of self-confidence and not simply roll over onto our backs in tough circumstances.**

Just to reiterate, I believe to have true confidence you must work diligently to attain strong conviction relating to a particular mispriced issue (or set of issues). Then, you must continually question and challenge that conviction as you hold the investment. You can't get overly attached to the positions in your book or the conviction levels you once had. What you loved yesterday, you must be prepared to sell today. It's imperative to avoid any emotional attachment no matter how much work you have done or how much you may like a company or a management team. This continual questioning of your thesis and expected outcome is key in avoiding the overconfidence trap.

An excellent example in wrestling of the confidence one should strive to attain is that of former Cornell wrestler Kyle Dake. From 2010-2013, Dake won four NCAA Division I national titles in four different weight classes, leading many to proclaim him as the greatest college wrestler of all time. (As a Cornell wrestling alum, you will certainly not get any disagreement from me.) Beyond Dake's high-level athletic skills and rigorous training, it's been said that he benefits from having confidence in essentially any position on the mat that he is in. Even more, he truly believes and wrestles as if each situation is "his position," which lends to his strengths and where he has the advantage over his opponent. Such an ideal competitive mindset is something we should also seek in investing. The goal of your diligence and persistence of your work should be to attain a level of confidence such that in every situation your appropriate response (to add, unwind, or hold on) is clairvoyant, decisive, and unwavering.

The Three Levels of Ignorance

As I see it, there are three basic levels of ignorance that hinder people in life, and particularly in investing. I believe it is important to be aware of these common shortfalls and to frequently question in which category you might unfortunately fall into. By gaining this understanding, you may be better able to identify and address areas of potential under- or overconfidence.

1) **You don't know what you don't know.** Donald Rumsfeld once called these issues the "unknown unknowns." This general unawareness relates to someone basically flying blind, who potentially gets lucky from time to time, but then does not

understand the basis of his or her good fortune. Having such oblivious ignorance often leads to an investor who is too aggressive and possibly overconfident as a result of random success.

2) **You know what you don't know.** This person has greater awareness and understands that there is a lot out there beyond his or her current knowledge base. This promotes investing that may be overly cautious, as the investor is overwhelmed and often intimidated by the issues and information beyond their understanding.

3) **Knowing it, but not being able to apply it.** On a broad level, this represents one of the largest issues in our society today, as detailed in the book "*The Check List Manifesto*" by Atul Gawande. Until recent decades, a primary shortcoming of mankind was not possessing the information to solve our problems. However, thanks to scientific discoveries and new technologies developed over the past century, we now have amassed a vast amount of that previously missing knowledge. Therefore, the main obstacle today is not attaining the knowledge, but knowing how to apply it.[1] This relates across numerous fields in our society, such as medicine, engineering, as well as investing. In today's environment of researching securities, we are buried with data, news stories, and various opinions that often overwhelm our minds and lead to confusion and indecision. The quest is how to most effectively sort through, retain, and apply that information to make the most educated and appropriate decisions for our portfolios.

Getting an Edge and Applying it

The ultimate means to gain confidence and conviction in one's ideas is to attain some sort of edge over the investing field. Unfortunately, the term "edge" has become almost taboo in recent years, as it holds negative investing connotations. This is mainly thanks to the actions of a small group of less-than-noble investors who decided to gain their edge through illegal or unethical means. That's not the type of edge I'm talking about here.

Instead, I view attaining an edge as congruent with our prior discussions of digging deep and developing a true understanding and perspective of the issues surrounding a company or industry. You can't get an edge from 50K feet, nor can you attain it by simply following the advice of others. In short, you get an edge through expanding the depth of your knowledge base and leveraging the extent of your work.

Gaining an edge can come by many routes, such as superior knowledge of a company or an industry, a better grasp of the financials and earnings sensitivities of a corporation, a greater understanding of the significance of an upcoming catalyst, or a past experience with a particular topic. This latter means was the source of one of my highest conviction ideas in recent years. And since I previously described one of my worst trades in Walter Energy, let me save some face here by walking through a more positive situation where I was able to profit from an edge I attained via my experience with a separate investment.

In mid-2012, I recognized the opportunity that the market was not appropriately punishing the shares of Royal Gold (NASDAQ: RGLD) for its large investment in Thompson Creek Metal's new Mount Milligan copper-gold project. In fact, Royal had actually outperformed its closest gold royalty peer Franco-Nevada (NYSE: FNV), which did not possess a similar near-term risk. So by going long Franco-Nevada and short Royal Gold, I was able to essentially cancel out the impact of changes in the gold price on either company and isolate the risk present to Royal.

Thompson Creek, a miner focused on the production of molybdenum (a steel hardening agent), announced it was acquiring Terrane Metals for $650 million on July 15, 2010. Terrane's main asset was a controversial copper-gold project in British Columbia, called Mount Milligan. Unfortunately, I remember the acquisition all too well, as my portfolio at the time was a major shareholder in Thompson Creek, whose shares were pounded as a result of the announcement. I am quite certain this was the most upset I've ever been at a management team…and I let them know about it (unfortunately to no avail). Prior to the acquisition announcement, shares of Thompson Creek had been hit already by lower molybdenum prices and from management discussing the possibility of making a large purchase of another mining company. But, instead of opportunistically buying back its own shares at depressed levels (my argument), management announced the intended acquisition, which in part was to be funded by using its depressed stock that they themselves had helped talk down! Talk about shooting yourself in the foot, then reloading and shooting the other foot.

The construction of Mount Milligan was a disaster, highlighted by capital expenditures that ultimately dwarfed original projections. I took a significant loss when I threw in the towel and sold my Thompson Creek shares. But fortunately, I did so prior to the first announcement of large cost overruns at the project, which I had correctly anticipated.

However, there was a bright side. My experience with Thompson Creek and Mount Milligan got me to notice Royal Gold's precarious position regarding its involvement with the project. Helping to fund Thompson Creek's acquisition of Terrane, Royal had announced simultaneously in 2010 that it was purchasing 25% of the gold stream in Mt. Milligan from Thompson Creek for the lessor of $400 million or the prevailing market price on 550,000 ounces of gold to be delivered to Royal. This was by far Royal's single largest investment in its history and a major departure from its smaller royalties, which had attracted investors mainly because they offered project diversification.

Like many other gold investors, I had liked the management team and the less-risky investment case surrounding Royal Gold. Cap ex inflation and mine start-up issues had become major problems for the industry. However, the royalty companies by their nature were not at risk to growing cap ex budgets or higher production costs and had spread their risks across a portfolio of mines. So it was puzzling to me why Royal Gold would stray from this model and invest such a large amount into what appeared to be a risky project.

On May 6, 2011, Thompson Creek announced that the capital budget for the Mt. Milligan project had increased by $350 million to $1.265 billion. Unfortunately, paying for this large bump was not a financial reality for Thompson Creek, who had just spent its excess cash on the acquisition of Terrrane. As such, Royal Gold, who already had $400 million in the pot, was essentially forced to ante-up and buy another 15% of the project's gold stream for $270 million in mid-2012.

At that time, it was becoming clear that Mt. Milligan was a mess and that any further construction cost increases would have to be funded by Royal. But it seemed this was not being recognized by the market. In mid-2012, Royal Gold shares were still benefiting from the strong price of gold and, in my view, not discounting the risk it had with Mt. Milligan. Royal's management argued that even under the potential event that Mt. Milligan was sold as part of a Thompson Creek bankruptcy, Royal would maintain the gold royalties it had purchased. Still, I knew that scenario would be messy and put into question if the mine would *ever* be built by an operator.

The price of gold began to fall in early October 2012. At that time, Royal began to underperform its gold peers (particularly Franco-Nevada), as the problems at Mt. Milligan were less overshadowed by the positive gold price and as Thompson Creek continued to struggle along. Royal's stock, which had peaked at over $100 per share in September 2012, fell into the low $40s by mid-2013. This was a significantly larger fall than experienced by Franco, which led to a strong return for my long-short pair trade. (Let me reiterate that this was an example of capitalizing on a mispriced issue at that time and not a reflection of any current views on these companies.)

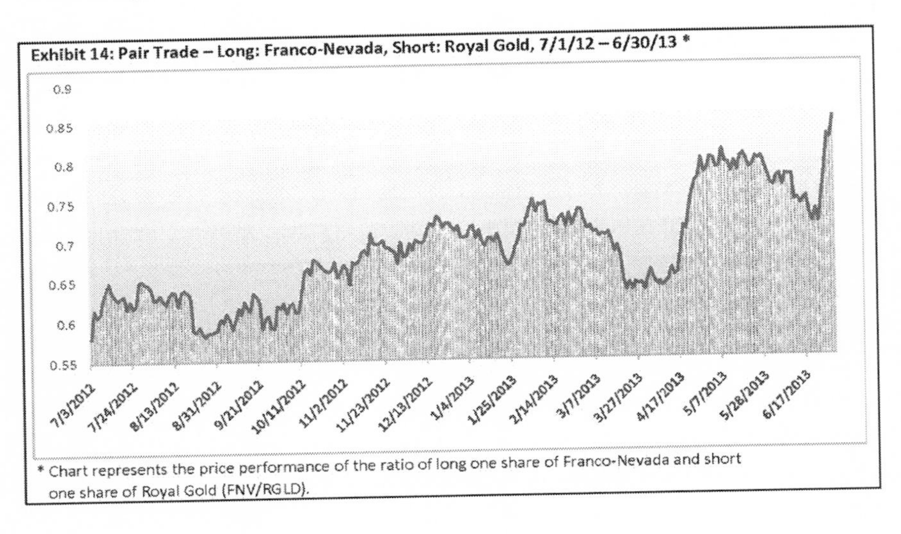

Exhibit 14: Pair Trade – Long: Franco-Nevada, Short: Royal Gold, 7/1/12 – 6/30/13 *

* Chart represents the price performance of the ratio of long one share of Franco-Nevada and short one share of Royal Gold (FNV/RGLD).

It Isn't About Trust

I want to highlight again the benefits that come from doing your own research and coming up with your own conclusion, rather than relying on the thoughts and work of others. A friend of mine who is a financial advisor once asked me,

"Who do you trust on the sell-side for research?"

"What do you mean by trust?" I replied.

"You know..which firm do you trust for investment ratings and targets?"

"Trust blindly?.. Oh gosh, no one. No one at all. It really doesn't work that way. It's my job to pick the stocks. I just use the Street for information and gaining a perspective. Not for their recommendations. I really couldn't care less about that."

That may have sounded arrogant, but those thoughts are shared by many institutional investors. Much of the time, the agenda for buy-siders just doesn't match up with those on the sell-side. Buy-side investors simply want to attain the information in order to get the price action correct or to help form their thesis for an investment. Conversely, sell-side firms have a large number of constituents to serve with various timelines and strategies. In fact, when I was a sell-side analyst, my firm once had a one-day research department off-site gathering, which included a panel discussion consisting of a group of our buy-side clients. The title of the session was "What the Buy-Side Wants." The comments from the panelists were interesting. However, it quickly became clear that they all wanted different things and different methods of service from our firm.

Also, the motivations among sell-siders are different than the buy-side. While being correct with their recommendations is important, the top concerns for sell-side analysts are getting votes for popular investor surveys and gaining credibility and respect from buy-side clients, which should translate into commission dollars for their firm. Additionally, an increasingly key role for analysts, and the sell-side in general, is providing corporate access for their institutional clients. That means setting up roadshows and conference meetings with clients and the management of the companies they cover. Unfortunately, companies are often biased to only allow sell-side analysts that have "Buy" ratings on their stock to set up those meetings. This tends to skew sells-side ratings more favorably, even with stocks analysts may not recommend otherwise.

On a very basic level, there are really only two types of jobs on Wall Street, those investing and those selling. Such simplicity is seldom recognized within the traditional brokerage house established order, and even begs the question why the sell-side has "Hold" ratings at all for the stocks they follow. Can you imagine a sales manager saying to the troops on the trading floor, "Now go out and generate those Hold tickets!?"

As discussed previously, company management teams are generally not trustworthy sources for opinions either. They typically have too much at stake and have invested too much time and money to be objective or to be forthright with their actual thoughts. For instance, it's interesting that corporate optimism is even evident during times of insider selling or during secondary offerings. In roadshow meetings prior to a secondary stock offering, I've often asked the management of a company the simple question, "If you're selling, why again should I be buying?" It's almost as if I'm being set-up for some kind of trap, like a Pink Panther movie when a mysterious person delivers a smoking bomb to the room of Inspector Clouseau. I can even picture Peter Sellers saying his classic line "It's a boom" when some secondaries are announced.

Secondary offerings and IPOs are commonly referred to as "deals" on Wall Street, which is often a tremendous misnomer. Many times an institutional salesperson has called me about a "deal" just announced by his or her firm. Frequently, my question back to them is something like, "Is this a 'deal' such as 50% off my sandwich at lunch, or a 'deal' like I give you five bucks and you kick me between the legs? Because if it's the latter, let's call it something else." Unfortunately, the sell-side really isn't motivated to help distinguish between the two, especially since they may be focused on getting struggling offerings to the finish line.

Prior to the pricing of an offering, you can typically get some level of feedback from the underwriters' syndicate desks, such as the offering being multiple times covered, or oversubscribed. But, many times you don't truly know the likelihood of success of the "deal" until it is priced and you receive your final share allocation. In positive situations, you generally get much fewer shares than you requested, which typically means the stock is likely to trade higher because the demand outweighs the amount of stock being offered. On the other hand, I've received calls from equity salespeople after the pricing saying, "Trip, your firm is such a valued client that we worked hard to get you the full allocation you requested." Oh no. Not good. That may be the biggest sell signal on Wall Street. Getting a full allocation had nothing to do with how good of a client my firm was. Rather, it related to demand for the offering being underwhelming and there being plenty of shares to go around. On those occasions, it's typically best to start selling immediately and just hope the stock price can hold up for long enough for you to get out of much of your position. That may sound too reactionary, but dumping the shares quickly might ease some of the inevitable pain, as the stock is almost certain to be hit from selling by other "special clients" (aka fellow suckers) with full allocations.

Let me be clear, I am not knocking the efforts of the sell-side or the needed set process surrounding stock offerings. We all have jobs to do and often families to feed. Nevertheless, stock offerings, particularly less popular ones, are frequently good examples of the misaligned objectives between the buy- and sell-side. Moreover, they also illustrate the need to question company management teams and their motivations.

All in all, strictly relying on the work of anyone other than yourself or your team will not provide you the solid knowledge base and conviction that is needed, especially when a position goes against you. When issues arise, you have to be able to defend your position by knowing you've read the documents, you've spoken to the experts, you know the numbers, you've done the work.

The Dark Side of Conviction

Once when I was having a difficult time in the market, a friend and fellow wiseass PM said to me, "Trip, it's real easy. Just overweight those trades that are going to make money and get rid of the bad ones." Ah, yes, so simple. Why hadn't I thought of that? Of course, the small problem was knowing exactly which positions in my book would end up being my best ideas and which were destined to be dogs. Sometimes the best ones are where you have the highest conviction, but sometimes not. Obviously, there are no guarantees, even with trades where it seems implausible that you could be wrong. Therefore, it's important not to get too comfortable with any position. Rather, you must be as skeptical with your highest conviction ideas as with the ones where you are most uncertain.

Take my latest experience with nickel. In early 2014, the price of nickel surged from roughly $14k per ton to over $19k due to the Indonesian government beginning to enforce a law that forbid the exports of unprocessed ore. The country was the largest global exporter of nickel concentrate, much of which was sent to China to supply its large stainless steel industry. (Nickel is a key ingredient in the production of stainless steel.) The new requirement stated that only refined exports of nickel would be allowed since Indonesia wanted the mining companies to build smelters in the country so that it could also capture proceeds related to the processing of the commodity. With Indonesia accounting for a major portion of the global export market, it seemed that an extremely tight nickel market was developing, which would drive the price much higher. In fact, even after the initial price bounce, a globally well-respected metals sell-side analyst titled a report, "Nickel Prices Up 25% in 2014 - You Ain't Seen Nothing Yet."

Given everything I had read about the nickel market, I agreed with this expectation for higher prices. Still, my real bullishness didn't develop until my aforementioned trip to China in 2014, where my group met with a large Chinese nickel pig iron producer. (Nickel pig iron uses laterite ores and serves as a substitute for pure nickel in the production of some grades of stainless steel. The Chinese nickel pig iron industry was largely formed as a reaction to a shortage of pure nickel in 2006-2007 and the resulting massive escalation in price, where the price for the most liquid 3-month contract on the LME rose approximately fourfold in slightly over a year.)

We traveled to the company's headquarters in the center of the Shandong Province to meet with the CEO. Our plant tour was canceled for the simple reason that the facility was idled because it had no available inventories of nickel concentrate to process. Adding to our general bullishness, in our meeting, the CEO expanded on the trade-related shortage of nickel, in particular his insight on the Indonesian government's determination to keep the ban in place and build a smelting industry, which would take several years. He then asked the hosting sell-side analyst about his nickel forecast. The analyst said that based on the prior shortage and ensuing price reaction, he thought the price could reach as high as $35k (up approximately another 80%) over the next year or two, to which the CEO said he was being too conservative. Too conservative?!! Wow, this was coming from a private-company executive who had no reason to mislead us and whose plant was not running because the company could not attain any nickel concentrate. How much deeper due diligence could I do? I couldn't imagine that many investors or analysts had traveled to BFE China to get this kind of insight! My conviction levels were suddenly near a max. After the meeting, our group giddily hurried back to the bus, with many of us eager to check how many hours until the European or US market open when we could place orders for nickel-related stocks. In hindsight, it was fortunate that there are not many sizeable pure plays on nickel in the equities market (stainless steel producers being the largest indirect play), and I rarely trade in the commodity market directly. Thus, I never attained a large nickel exposure despite my high conviction.

Surprisingly to me and many others, the upward move in nickel prices began to fade shortly after my China trip, as supplies were boosted by increased low-grade nickel concentrate exports from the Philippines and apparent underreporting of nickel inventories elsewhere in China. Also, an import tariff by the European Union on Chinese stainless steel was a drag on nickel demand. Finally, and maybe most importantly, macro factors (slowing Chinese GDP and a stronger US dollar) provided large headwinds to all metals, including nickel. As shown in the following exhibit, the result has been a dramatic fall in nickel prices since mid-2014. All in all, my experience with nickel reminded me that I needed to be critical of even my highest conviction ideas, particularly when opposed by macroeconomic factors. Having high conviction levels should still be our goal, but it shouldn't prevent us from scrupulously questioning those ideas on a constant basis.

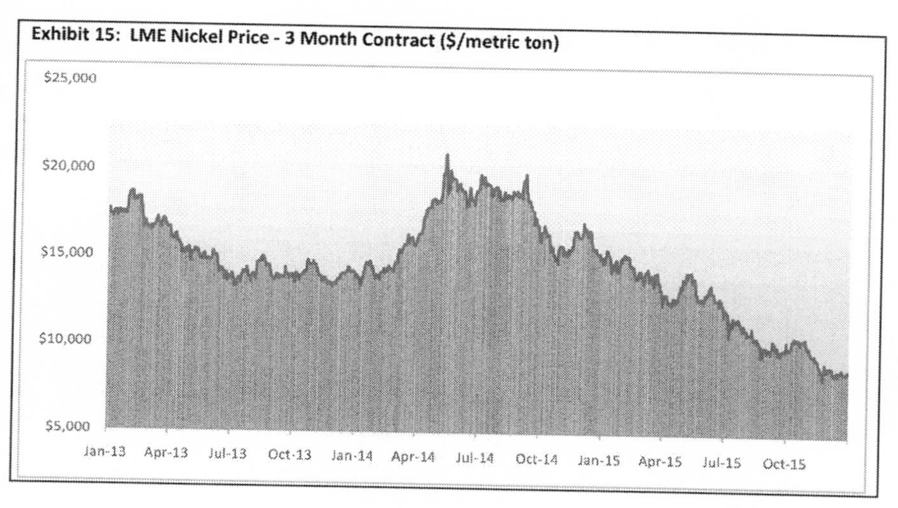

Exhibit 15: LME Nickel Price - 3 Month Contract ($/metric ton)

Believing Your Own BS

Several years ago, I started saying about people who were highly convinced of their ideas that they "believed their own BS." I've tended to use it when someone emphatically verbalizes thoughts that seem on the extreme side or even ridiculous. In many cases, the person with the opinion acts as if there is no way they could be wrong. Management teams, talk show hosts, sell-side analysts (some), and politicians are frequent offenders here. Such people tend to express an extreme level of confidence with *all* their ideas. Naturally, they can come across as a bit pompous, making them a bit difficult to be around. You know the type.

Still, as painful as they may be at times, I've learned something about people who "believe their own BS." They are frequently very successful. While what they are saying may sound obnoxious or at a minimum off the mark, their high conviction can often trump (excuse the pun of someone who seems to fit the mold here) what may be a shortfall in substance. This brings people to their side who are hesitant to oppose the person's stance since "they have so much confidence in what they are saying."

Of course, I'm not advocating falling back into the overconfidence trap. But in investing, "believing your own BS" can have some merits. For instance, it might prevent you from being shaken out of a position when the price action or sentiment is against you. Or it may allow you to convince your boss why your thesis on a stock still holds. "Believing your own BS" doesn't have to be negative. Nor must it be controversial, arrogant, and unappreciative of opposing ideas. In the best case, it should relate to someone with high self-esteem and a humble belief in themselves. I rather like being around such individuals.

Pete: *Wait a minute. Who elected you leader of this outfit?*

Ulysses Everett McGill *(played by George Clooney): Well Pete, I figured it should be the one with the capacity for abstract thought. But if that ain't the consensus view, then hell, let's put it to a vote.*

Pete: *Suits me. I'm voting for yours truly.*

Ulysses Everett McGill: *Well I'm voting for yours truly too.*

[Everett and Pete look at Delmar for the deciding vote.]

Delmar O' Donnell: *Okay…I'm with you fellas.*

Movie: O Brother, Where Art Thou?

Chapter 7:

An MBA from the University of Common Sense

I recently watched a story on *The NBC Nightly News* regarding a disturbing trend in automobile-train related accidents. According to the story, an increasing number of accidents are occurring due to people blatantly driving around railroad crossing guards and being hit by oncoming locomotives.[1] I would guess these individuals are not thrill-seekers trying to get a rush by narrowly beating the train over the tracks. Rather, they are likely impatient (and ignorant!) drivers ignoring any shred of reason in order to get to their destination in a more prompt manner.

Unfortunately, this probably says something not so positive about our society in general. Are we really that stupid and obtuse? Are we so driven by our type-A personalities that we forget all logic? We are the generation that created the internet, that are finding incredible cures for illnesses that have plagued humanity for centuries, and that are sending probes to observe distant planets. Yet, we don't have, or won't listen to, the common sense that says you shouldn't risk playing bumper cars with an oncoming train.

This lack of reasoning reminds me of an impatient woman I observed on an American Airlines flight many years ago from New York LaGuardia to Dallas-Ft. Worth (LGA-DFW). Before takeoff, the stewardess informed the cabin that because of strong headwinds, we would be landing in St. Louis to refuel before going on to DFW. Most passengers seemed to understand that and had no issue with the necessary stop. However, one woman threw a fit, squabbling with the stewardess that she's flown American for 20 years and has never been on a New York-Dallas flight that had to refuel. Looking around, I could tell most everyone near me on the plane was thinking the same thing..."First off lady, the vast majority of adults in this country have also probably flown American for 20 years or more. And second, fine, maybe you haven't been on a LGA-DFW flight when it has had to refuel. But would you rather us risk it by not refueling in St. Louis and seeing if we can make it in to Dallas on the fumes? Do you have any common sense at all?"

At these moments, there has to be some disconnect in the minds of such people that ignores what they know as the basic "do's and don'ts" and follows an illogical decision path driven by their emotions and egos. What they instinctively know as the correct move or thought is superseded by the importance they place on an event or subject matter (such as being on time). If the woman really pondered about it for a bit, maybe she would conclude that she was being highly irrational and that refueling and being late to land in DFW was the "no-brainer" choice.

Common sense isn't a difficult concept. It's not something you go to school for, learn on the job, or is a critical section of a certification exam. For example, I don't remember anyone ever having to specifically tell me not to go around the railroad crossing guards. Moreover, common sense isn't something that's going to impress others when you show you have it. ("*Hey man, smart move for stopping before that oncoming train.*") But, it is something that will likely be noticed by many when you demonstrate a lack of it.

Finance and investment management can be complex subjects. There are thousands of intellectually-challenging books and articles on these broad topics, many of which also dive deeply into other complex subject matters like mathematics, economics, and policy analysis. So, like many professions, there is an abundance of knowledge and information available to money managers and analysts, much of what is required to know in order to do these jobs effectively. Still, while striving to attain and apply this wisdom, a major fault of many investors seems to boil down to an inability to follow common sense. It's that simple. Whether they get swept up by the emotions of the day or they make a topic more complex than it really is, PMs often seem to ignore basic intuition and make decisions that are in direct contradiction to what a sensible investor would conclude. This mental separation between their actions and what should be the obvious choice ends up being a key detriment to their performance, offsetting what may be very intellectual work and thought behind a position.

Some of my best friends are institutional equity salespeople. So I try not to poke *too much* fun at those with that job. In all seriousness, the vast majority of salespeople I've worked with are hard-working, knowledgeable individuals who serve their clients well. Nevertheless, a couple of comments and questions I've heard from salespeople over the years are just too good not to share, and to me are decent examples of a lapse in common sense, especially for people that make a living from the securities market. My favorite could be when a salesperson asked a member of my team if he was having a terrible day. "No, not particularly. Should I be?" he responded. "Well, didn't one of your long positions just undergo a 2-for-1 stock split?" the salesperson asked. The salesperson's thinking was that the investment was now suddenly worth half as much as the day before since the stock price was cut in half. She ignored, or was not aware of, the well-known fact that with the 2:1 stock split, the number of shares outstanding of the company doubled and that we now owed twice as many shares. Thus, the value of our position was unchanged. I think my team member was a little lost for words on how to respond to that one.

To be fair, let's just say that the salesperson got her job despite not taking any finance or securities classes along the way, and that she didn't realize the shares outstanding of the company would double with the split. But, did she really think the board of directors of the corporation would voluntarily make an announcement that would cut in half the company's equity value? That seems like a pretty easy one to me.

On another occasion, a salesperson called me about a $5 stock that "obviously" had little downside. "Yep, only 100% downside," the smartass in me responded. After giving me what I guess was the obligatory chuckle, the salesman went on to point out that the market cap of the stock was now below $300 million and the business was *surely* worth more than that! I was not familiar with the company and didn't disagree with him at first. However, as I pulled up the balance sheet on my Bloomberg terminal, I fired back, "Did you happen to notice this company has over $2 billion in debt?" (Long silence on his end)…..Then finally, "Yeah, but look! It's all short-term debt. It'll be gone soon." (Long silence now on my end)… "Oh, yes, it probably will be gone soon, along with your $300 million of market cap…You know, I really better go." Seriously? These are people whose jobs are to converse with clients that manage billions of dollars. How could he really think such a thing?

Maybe the salesperson did not understand that the enterprise value of the company included both the market capitalization and total of the outstanding debt. But, I do think it's a bit of common sense to know that debt, whether short- or long-term, cannot just magically disappear by no actions or with no consequences for the company.

I'm sure I'm being a bit unfair with these examples. Those individuals are not as oblivious as their comments suggest. It's likely just a matter of not really thinking before asking a question or making a comment. And we've all done that before. (This is coming from a guy who when once buying a gift certificate for a wedding gift answered "catholic" when asked "what denomination?") Therefore, one element of common sense is remembering to think before you speak. As Abraham Lincoln famously said, "Better to remain silent and thought a fool than to speak up and remove all doubt."

Common Sense Principles to Investing

The following are some common sense principles that I believe should be very evident to investors of all sorts. Granted, some are more intuitive than others. Also, some transcend the arena of investing and are applicable to life in general. In any case, to serious investors and analysts, I believe knowing and practicing these basic common sense tenets should be essentially second-nature.

Common Sense Principle #1: Common sense can be contrarian.

On the face of it, this doesn't seem right. Does this mean the entire crowd at times is neglecting common sense and not appropriately viewing a situation? Could the majority of the investing field be off-track in their assessment of the market or of a particular sector or company? The answer is undoubtedly "yes," and there are numerous examples to illustrate.

Some of the clearest cases of common sense not being with the consensus has occurred during market bubbles. In particular, the dot-com bubble of the late 1990s and early 2000s was in hindsight an obvious period of irrational optimism toward many new, unproven companies in the technology space. Sure, not listening to common sense was very profitable for dot-com investors for much of that time, as almost any stock associated with the internet or technology soared to exaggerated levels. On the sell-side at that time, I remember getting into an elevator with an associate analyst with our firm's team that followed internet stocks. In the brief three-floor journey to the cafeteria, she made an inconsequential comment in passing about a dot-com company. Without hearing anything else or knowing anything at all about the company, I immediately went back to my desk and bought the stock in my personal account. Now how's that for due diligence?! Like most everything in the sector, the stock went to the moon...of course, only to plummet back to earth with the bursting of the tech bubble. Sadly, too many people have similar stories from this period. Like me, they bought stocks knowing nothing and ignoring any investment discipline because they got caught up in the technology hype and market craze at the time, only to ride the stocks back down when the bubble deflated.

The dot-com period was an exciting time for investing, with analysts pondering the seemingly endless potential of the internet and how this new-found world would lead to new innovative companies that would emerge and change our lives. For an investor, it was like shooting fish in a barrel. The common view on Wall Street was that anyone who dared question the future of the sector or the stocks' valuations really "didn't understand technology or where we were all headed." In fact, I remember one of our analysts publishing a research note on an internet company that basically said he could find no valuation metric that justified the lofty price of the stock, but that he was still maintaining his "Buy" rating because it was just obvious that the stock was going higher. As crazy as it sounds, that appeared like a sensible position at the time, and maybe that stock did keep rising for a while longer. But, in looking back, it's quite obvious the call, as well as the overall jubilance toward the sector at that time, went against what should have been common sense investing.

Unfortunately, I was a tech analyst wannabe and was subjected to following stocks in the housing and building materials sector at that time. When I spoke on the morning research call, I would normally get about two minutes of airtime, typically just after a technology analyst would talk for 15 or 20 minutes about pets.com or a similar now-nonexistent company. Still, my dramatically less glamorous life following boring old economy stocks presented me the opportunity to practice common sense by recognizing the irrational optimism also at that time involving another group of companies, the manufactured housing industry, also known as trailer stocks. (I guess it shouldn't have been a big surprise when I couldn't get much speaking time on the morning call.)

In the early and mid-1990s, U.S. shipments of manufactured housing grew dramatically, expanding at a 16% annual rate from 1991 to 1996.[2] Reasons most often cited for the growth were the affordability of factory-built homes versus site-built houses, their enhanced quality (with double- and triple-wide units becoming the norm), increased usage as second homes, and more attractive communities in which to place the homes. As such, there emerged large demand for more plants to build manufactured homes, as well as more retail centers to sell the homes. Manufacturing and retail companies in the industry were in their heyday, and the stocks of the publicly-traded companies soared throughout most of the 1990s. Of course, it helped that the overall stock market was also in a distinct bull market for the vast majority of that period.

In early 1999, I had been working as an associate research analyst in Austin, Texas, but I had recently accepted a job in New York City to be a lead analyst at a major investment bank. My girlfriend (later wife) was still in Austin, and so I made many trips back to Texas at that time. In doing so, I frequently traveled the highway connecting downtown Austin to the new airport east of the city. The road was littered with manufactured housing retail dealers, some rather dingy, but others more landscaped and upscale. Most were offering terms like "zero down" or making aggressive statements on large billboards such as "no application rejected." Each time I visited, it seemed that one or two new dealerships had popped up. Finally, on one visit, after counting up to nearly 20 retail dealers on that one stretch of highway, I concluded that it had all become way overdone. I had followed the manufactured housing group as an associate analyst for several years, and had bought into the pitch that the industry had emerged from shabby trailers to an attractive alternative to low-end sight-built housing. But the excess now seemed ridiculous. There just couldn't be this much true demand.

When I got back to New York, I started digging more into the industry, particularly the financing aspect of the business. After talking to many sources, it increasingly became evident to me that the industry was a house of cards built on extremely easy credit terms to the consumer. Loans were being made (and then securitized) to individuals with very low FICA scores, a credit statistic unknown to much of Wall Street at that time. (Remember, this was prior to the bursting of the more significant site-built housing bubble in the late 2000s.) The problem was that historically manufactured housing buyers with poor credit tended to default between years three to five of the mortgage. And thanks to the aggressive tactics of the lending companies, many of these $50K (or less)-priced homes were now being financed over 20 or 30 years! For a depreciating asset nonetheless! It goes without saying, the likelihood of many buyers to stay current on their mortgage throughout that lengthy period was fairly remote. But, lenders knew they could pass on the buck by selling the low-quality mortgages in bundles through the securitization market, a practice that was greatly exposed with the bursting of the overall housing bubble approximately a decade later.

By 1999 and early 2000, mortgage defaults for manufactured homes were starting to pile up. As a result, the finance companies cut back on lending, which in turn forced many retailers out of business. The vast majority of independent retailers had floorplan financing agreements that required, in the event of foreclosure, any unsold inventory to be bought back by the manufacturers, a clause called "repurchase obligations" that not many investors or analysts had ever paid attention to in the footnotes of the public fillings. It all began to quickly unravel, resulting in a dramatic fall in industry shipments in the following years, as well as the bankruptcy of many of the publicly-traded companies.

Exhibit 16: US Manufactured Home Shipments (thousand homes), 1980-2014

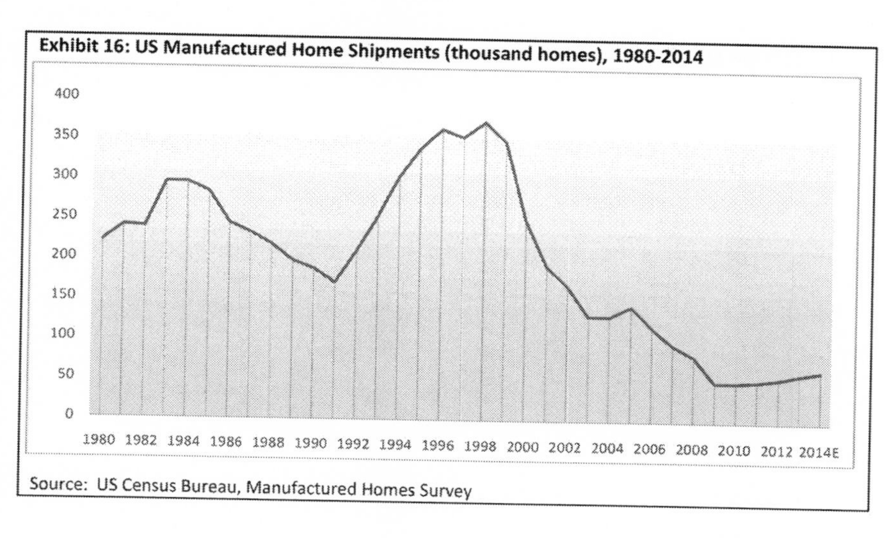

Source: US Census Bureau, Manufactured Homes Survey

My contrarian call to downgrade the manufactured housing group in mid-1999 was probably the best call of my career. It's too bad that I was only 27 years old and had no real credibility at the time. Still, I knew I was on the right track when a CEO of one of the major companies called and yelled at me because of my downgrade. The next week that particular stock plummeted when the company announced that its largest independent retail customer had defaulted and it would have to repurchase nearly 2,000 homes, leading to a large charge to its earnings.

Unfortunately, not all my upgrades and downgrades as a sell-side analyst worked out this well. Nevertheless, I really credit this particular call to simply stepping back, objectively considering the situation, and asking questions regarding what was really driving the industry. In hindsight, after seeing all those retail dealerships in Austin, it was just common sense.

Common Sense Principle #2: Risk doesn't have to be so complex.

The topic of risk is one of the most discussed subjects in financial textbooks and journals. This is appropriately so, as controlling risk exposure is an extremely critical function of a portfolio manager. In fact, several large hedge funds refer to the heads of their portfolios as "Risk Managers," rather than "Portfolio Managers," highlighting the importance of the topic.

Despite valiant efforts to define risk in the educational system, the academic versions of risk often fall short in defining true risk in the market. The 2014 book *"The Pillars of Finance"* by Guy Fraser-Sampson discusses at length the shortcomings of the academic definitions of risk, especially as it relates to low probability events. The book insightfully challenges the preconceptions of risk and how it relates to returns.[3]

Undoubtedly, defining risk and measuring returns with respect to risk are key elements to portfolio management. Still, I firmly believe that considering the day-to-day influences of various risks to one's portfolio doesn't necessarily have to be complicated or calculated numerically. In short, there is a common sense element to risk. Whether it is event risk relating to an earnings release, financial risk relating to a bank note, counter-party risk relating to an operating agreement, market risk relating to securities in general, or the numerous other forms of risk, I tend not to need a textbook or complex equation to identify it. Instead, risk is often like the famous saying about pornography, "I can't always define it, but I know it when I see it."

In reality, risk is everywhere, when you step out of your house, when you drive your car, or when you buy a stock. It's unavoidable. It's the probability you assign to the risk factor and the potential downside from the risk that matters. For instance, most of us fly on commercial airplanes despite the very adverse effects that would be imposed on us from a plane crash. We know the probability of a crash is very small. Hence, our apprehension is generally low when we fly. Similarly, when you buy a blue chip stock with a long track record and a sound balance sheet, you assess the probability of an extreme negative occurrence (e.g., bankruptcy) also as very low. It's not that the risk is zero. Fraser-Sampson would argue there is some probability for a blue chip company to go belly-up (like Enron). But we are generally comfortable with taking that risk.

On the other hand, one should feel very uncomfortable buying a stock of a company carrying a large debt load when industry conditions are quickly deteriorating. It should be similar to the nervousness we would feel getting onto a single-engine plane flying into a hurricane. The probability of a crash goes up dramatically.

Thus, I believe a common sense principle in investing is not to rely on defining risk solely by a calculated number, but to also follow your intuition and to constantly and proactively identify and evaluate the numerous risks to your portfolio. Use your apprehension and nervousness as an internal risk gauge. There is nothing wrong with following your non-numeric gut feel in the process. It should play an important part in your overall risk assessment.

Common Sense Principle #3: Things change (including companies).

For much of my life the New England Patriots were awful and typically finished near the bottom of their division in the NFL. As a kid, neither I, nor most people, would have dreamed the Patriots would become the dominant team of recent decades, winning four Super Bowl Championships in the past 14 years, including three out of four from 2002 to 2005. But with new players, new coaches, and rejuvenated fans, the new Patriots had no real connection to the team's dismal past. There really was no reason why they had to continue on their losing track. Circumstances change, teams change, companies and sectors change.

I think this principle is an easy one. Common sense tells us that you can't count on conditions to remain the same over time, be it in football, your hometown, or the fundamentals surrounding a company. Solely relying on historic knowledge of a corporation, stock charts, or past statistics is a recipe for underperformance.

A former superior of mine used to have confidence in a well-known, sell-side valuation program that was driven by a company's prior financial performance. When I was discussing a stock, he would listen but then often point to a green dot on a chart generated by the program that illustrated the company's estimated intrinsic value based on its prior ten years of operating data. Sure, that was interesting to examine in a few cases. But, in several instances, my comeback would be something like, "That's fine. But this is a dramatically different company today. They've made a number of transformative acquisitions, the industry has drastically changed, management is different, they've spun off bad businesses, and their balance sheet has been completely restructured. Basing the valuation of the company on rear-view mirror metrics is completely inappropriate." Basically, the green dot was irrelevant. And frankly, the notion that it superseded my understanding of the company was insulting to the hard work I had put into the idea and often my long history following the stock. I can only imagine what Old Man Market would tell him to do with the green dot.

Common Sense Principle #4: Stop dwelling on your losses.

I'm truly amazed by the composure of many professional golfers. After missing a three-foot putt for par, seldom do they lose their temper by throwing a club or shouting obscenities. Rather, they are typically able to keep their emotions in check and regroup for the tee-shot on the next hole. They put the bad behind them and move forward.

Unfortunately, in my athletic career, I had a harder time letting go of disappointments. I would often sulk for days after a big wrestling loss. Still, over time, the pain of losing would fade and I would focus on more positive outcomes. A few years ago, my college coach was doing some office cleaning and found a couple old tapes of my matches, which he sent to me. My wife and kids were not extremely excited about watching them when they arrived in the mail. So late one night when everyone was asleep, I found an old VHS player, popped in one of the tapes, and began watching a match from my sophomore year. While I was watching, I realized I couldn't remember if I had won or lost the competition. As such, I started to really get into the match, yelling at myself on the screen competing approximately 20 years prior. Toward the end of the match, I made a poor move, which my opponent capitalized on, and I lost. After watching it, I was livid. What a terrible performance! How could I make such a dumb mistake? It took me a while to calm down and realize the ridiculousness of my anger at midnight so many years later. I had effectively and fortuitously forgotten about that defeat. Hopefully, I had learned something from it at the time, but I had long moved on and put it in my past. There was certainly no point in reliving it now. I put away the tapes deep in the attic and haven't brought them out since. I much prefer the more positive outcomes that I have held on to in my memories.

There is typically nothing to be gained from dwelling on past failures. What's done is done. We must learn from our mistakes and then not let them hinder us, or our confidence, as we move onward. In the securities business, dwelling on prior poor investments is generally a waste of energy and prevents you from giving your best efforts on the rest of your positions.

> *"Brethren, I do not regard myself as having laid hold of it yet; but one thing I do: forgetting what lies behind and reaching forward to what lies ahead."*
>
> *Philippians 3:13 (NIV)*

Common Sense Principle #5: Quit thinking the market has to make sense.

Old Man Market may be sensible and all-knowing over time, but in the short term he's often erratic, inconsistent, and even gullible. There's no other way to explain it. The large price moves in some securities on trivial matters or particularly on whimsical market rumors frequently seem illogical. Many times, I've been surprised by a dramatic move in a stock on a rumor that I viewed as extremely farfetched. Often these events involved companies that I knew better than the average investor, so maybe the possibility seemed less extraordinary to the overall market. Still, I'm frequently amazed there are enough, dare I say, "suckers" that buy into the nonsense and help push intra-day prices to extreme levels.

There are examples of this practically every day in the market. But one that comes to mind is the price action on April 11, 2007 in Gold Fields Ltd (NYSE: GFI), a large South African gold miner whose ADR trades actively on the New York Stock Exchange. On that day, GFI rose as much as 11% on large volume due to a Bloomberg article reporting speculation that an investor named Edward Pastorini was planning to lead a group that would make a cash and share offer for the company, which then had a sizable market cap of $12.5 billion.[4,5,6,7]

To investors like me who were familiar with Gold Fields, the article came as a major surprise. GFI was in the midst of significant operating problems at many of its key mines, which were plagued by labor, safety, and geological issues. As such, it seemed unlikely that anyone (even the other large gold companies) would have the desire or capacity to pay such a large sum given the troubles at the company. Moreover, details of the plan seemed very fuzzy. No one had ever heard of Edward Pastorini, nor his group that claimed to have $2 billion in "funds," including cash, stock in other large gold companies, and bullion. Also, his plan to somehow buy, or take control of, the company with this relatively small amount and then sell-off the pieces made little sense and seemed quite implausible to anyone doing the math. After the morning spike in the stock and as more updates of the article were released, investors began to scrutinize the speculation and conclude the absurdness of the claim. The stock finally retreated and finished up only slightly for the session.

In the days following the speculation, little else surfaced about the rumor or Edward Pastorini (whose name was only familiar because it shared the surname name with former NFL quarterback, Dan Pastorini). The New York Post reported later to having discussions with the mystery man through emails, in which he adamantly claimed his existence as a major gold investor. In any case, the matter cooled off quickly and was seen as a farce in the gold industry within days. Still, if it was so illogical and farfetched to the average gold bug, why the large initial reaction in GFI's stock price? How could Old Man Market in all his wisdom be so susceptible to such a scam?

Seeking the answer to this question, as well as the unexpected short-term price action with many securities, is futile in my view. Reasons could involve manipulation, crowdedness on one side of the trade, antsy short-term shareholders, overly-aggressive event players, or simply a large investor with urgency to complete an order. In many cases, you just have to accept that you will never know the answer. All in all, Old Man Market can act a bit senile at times, and so common sense should tell us not to expect him to seem logical every day.

Common Sense Principle #6: There is no good or bad luck.

My wife's uncle is one of my favorite people to be around, particularly as few individuals are as impassioned about certain topics as he is. The University of Oklahoma football is one of those topics. In fact, he gets into watching the games so intensely that if things are not going well for the team, he often believes it's partially his fault, or worse his wife's fault. Some element has to change. Either everyone must switch seats or his wife needs to go shopping and quit watching the game. Without doing his part, the Sooners are doomed to fail.

I laugh when I picture him rearranging the seats in front of the TV. But, admittedly, I also have been known to fall into superstitious tendencies. Several years ago, daughter, who was five-years old at the time, gave me one of those funny-shaped rubber bands to wear on my wrist. Suddenly, Daddy started to make a lot of money at work. (Thank you sweetheart.) So I wore the rubber band for weeks, and when its powers started to wear off, I asked my daughter if she had a new one for me. My co-workers probably thought I had lost my mind.

On another occasion, I noticed that I had a terrible losing streak in the market on days that I wore short-sleeved shirts. That's a real bummer of a trend when you're working in a casual-attire office in Dallas in the middle of the hot summer. Unfortunately, my bad luck with short-sleeved shirts soon spilled over to long-sleeved shirts as well. My conclusion was that I either wear no shirt to work, or maybe I should take a harder look at the positions driving the returns in my portfolio rather than focusing on my wardrobe.

Of course, the idea of good luck or bad luck charms and rituals is irrational. We tend to create them to support a trend or tendency that we don't understand or can't explain. Common sense tells us that it amounts to a lot of wasted energy.

Nevertheless, let's not dismiss it all. There may be some value to our superstitions. If a good luck charm or routine provides some boost to your confidence, there is obviously a benefit to it. For instance, hockey goalies are some of the most superstitious people in sports. Many have a pre-game ritual that they follow religiously in warm-ups, which they truly believe helps their play. Quite honestly, if it enhances their confidence, it might. As discussed earlier, having confidence in any important activity, especially investing, is critical. Therefore, something that may boost one's confidence, particularly in tough times, should be viewed as a positive, even as silly as it may seem. On that thought, I think I'll check if my daughter has any new rubber bands.

Common Sense Principle #7: Stop expecting to win every day.

If I could have a quarter for the number of times in my career someone answered "frustrated" when I've asked them how they were doing, I would…

well, have a lot quarters. People in this business tend to have little patience, especially in the short term-focused hedge fund arena. We unrealistically want our ideas to work every day, and when they are not working or when we can't make sense of the price action, we get irritated. This expectation is obviously irrational.

Unless you're day trading, you must come to grips with the idea that each day does not have to be a step in the right direction. As much as we may wish it were the case, returns typically are not linear. Your portfolio is likely to have some "two steps forward and one step back" action...or more realistically something like 4 steps forward, 3 steps back, 7 steps forward, 5 steps back, etc.

The most successful major league baseball team in recent decades (the team that had the best regular season record and also won the World Series) was the 1998 New York Yankees, with a regular season record of 114-48. The superstar-filled team, which included Derek Jeter, Bernie Williams, David Cone, Andy Pettitte, and Mariano Rivera, will undoubtedly go down as one of the best in baseball history. But they still lost 48 games. That's 30% of the games they played.[8] And they are still considered the best! Stop being frustrated that every day in the market is not a victory. It doesn't have to be.

> *"A good friend of mine used to say, 'This is a very simple game. You throw the ball, you catch the ball, you hit the ball. Sometimes you win, sometimes you lose, sometimes it rains.'"*
>
> *Ebby Calvin LaLoosh, movie: Bull Durham*

Common Sense Principle 8: Don't forget the basics.

One thing I love about wrestling is that the basic moves you learn in the beginning are the same fundamental moves that can be used at any age and even at the highest level of competition. Once a week, I am the coach/ chaos manager for my son's Kindergarten through 2nd grade wrestling team. The kids are pretty adorable learning the sport at that age, albeit with the typical attention spans of a cluster of gnats. Nevertheless, when the other coaches and I are able to briefly capture their focus, one of the first moves we teach them is a basic drop-step for a double leg takedown. It's one of the core penetration skills and can be used throughout their wrestling careers. In fact, it is essentially the same go-to move that Jordan Burroughs used to win a gold medal for the USA at 2012 Olympics in London. (His is generally referred to as a "blast double.")

Likewise, in investing, focusing on the basics can be key. It is important to keep in mind the core fundaments of a company or an industry, which can be the year-after-year driving factor behind an investment. In particular, I've frequently focused on identifying advantageous industry structures, as detailed in step one of the due diligence process in Chapter 3. A company can go through various challenges, but in the end, it's often the favorable structure of its industry, or its position within the industry, that ultimately wins out over short-term issues and remains the key investment theme. An excellent example is the U.S. aggregates industry. (Aggregates are simply rocks and sand which are key ingredients to concrete and asphalt, and are also used in applications such as road base.) Demand for aggregates naturally goes through ups and downs due to the cyclicality of construction activity. Nevertheless, the major U.S. producers (Vulcan Materials, Martin Marietta Materials, CRH plc, Summit Materials) for years have enjoyed consistent and favorable pricing given the local nature of the business. This is largely due to the high transportation costs of aggregates relative to the value of the product and the companies' high market shares in many geographies. In my experience, betting on companies with such fundamental tailwinds is typically a keen and profitable approach, especially when those stocks are being punished for transitory issues.

Common Sense Principle #9: Don't trust the crowd.

One of the most heartbreaking, yet little known, stories in sports is that of an accomplished Virginia high school wrestler named Casey Graham. On February 23, 1986, Graham was wrestling for his fourth high school state championship in a fieldhouse at James Madison University. With a 15-6 lead in the final match, he was soon to become the state's 13th ever four-time state champion. With 10 seconds left on the clock, the crowd began to count down the time. Tragically, the crowd's count was too quick and got ahead of the actual clock. Graham, listening to the crowd and not watching the clock, rolled to his back and raised four fingers when the crowd's count hit zero. This gave his opponent a moment's opportunity to flop on top of him and pin him with one second left on the actual clock, winning the match! Amazingly, Graham showed incredible sportsmanship, by keeping his composure, quietly getting up, and shaking his opponent's hand, an act that was later recognized by the Virginia governor.[9]

Honestly, I'm not sure I could have handled it that well. But I am confident that trusting the crowd is a definite way to end up on your back, both in athletics and in investing. Yes, the roar of the crowd can be enthralling and enticing to follow, but it can also lead you down the wrong path and disconnect you from your thoughts and beliefs. As such, you should constantly consider how your thoughts are being shaped by the crowd (e.g., sell-side research, the financial media, your peers in the business, etc.) and seek to connect with your own opinions and expectations.

Common Sense Principle #10: Know what you are getting into and have an escape plan.

This is probably going to sound somewhat stereotypical for rural life in Oklahoma. But one summer in my youth, my older cousin volunteered to be a storm chaser for the local radio station. To his credit, it was a valiant effort to liven up what was a pretty dull summer in a small town. To make it a surprise, he had not told me about this new hobby until he picked me up one evening and was driving alongside a stretch of farmland looking up at the clouds. Fortunately for us, we didn't see any twisters or anything else to make the news at the local station (which wouldn't have taken much). However, I did learn a little bit about storm chasing. One key tip was that, when viewing a storm, you should place yourself at the intersection of two country roads. This gives you the option of escaping a tornado in any direction should one head your way. Again, I was very happy that I didn't have to apply this new knowledge.

Suffice it to say that my storm chasing days did not last long, as I thought of good excuses not to accompany my cousin on further expeditions. Still, looking back at the experience, I think there are a couple parallel investing lessons to be drawn here. First, unlike me jumping into my cousin's car headed for the dark skies, you should always know what you are getting into when investing. Stocks can be risky investments. There is nothing guaranteed. Shareholders are the last in line in the event of a liquidation, thus making their investment generally the most volatile part of a company's capitalization structure.

Unfortunately, the riskiness of stocks is often forgotten during bull market periods. At those times, in a lack of discipline, investors tend underappreciate the numerous idiosyncratic and macro risks inherent to all equities. They often get sloppy with their research and, due to the recent market performance, they irrationally expect every stock they buy to head even higher and return a nice profit. Conversely, you must avoid this blindly optimistic view of your positions and be constantly reverent to the risks of your investments, particularly for troubled companies. For instance, don't be surprised by large volatility when you purchase a high beta small cap stock or a highly-leveraged company dependent on one variable or key event. Again, remember that these are stocks, not annuities. The investment journey with equities can be very bumpy, so you must always be prepared for some adverse weather.

Second, leave yourself options. Similar to viewing a storm from an intersection, you want to have an escape plan if conditions get dicey. Of course, with stocks, an investor typically has the option of quickly escaping danger by selling the investment in the market. I even remember being in a one-on-one company meeting that was going so poorly that I couldn't stand owning the stock one more minute. So I faked needing a bathroom break in order to make a quick call to my trader to sell the stock. Still, there are many cases with illiquid or nonpublic investments that severely restrict one's options. Investors should be very cognizant of those situations, as the ability to avoid the oncoming storm may be limited.

Common Sense Principle #11: Take only good shots.

From my experience, the biggest step-up from high school to Division I college wresting is the increased difficulty in finishing offensive moves, or shots (commonly known as single legs, double legs, high C's), for a takedown at the college level. In high school, good wrestlers generally score on a high percentage of the shots they take on their opponent. However, the higher level of defensive skills by most college wrestlers means that at that level, once you get in on your opponent's legs, the fight has often just begun. As such, I quickly learned in college the importance of not flailing around and wasting energy with unproductive shots. Rather, to score on good competition, wrestlers must set up their shots and be deliberate in their timing and effort.

This is similar in investing. Making too many investments with half-hearted research or without a solid thesis is typically a recipe for underperformance. As mentioned previously, without the foundation of focused due diligence and a thorough understanding of the trade, you will generally not be able to attain the conviction level required to adequately deal with the trade if things go poorly. Thus, you must be deliberate when initiating your positions and only take calculated, well-planned "shots" at opportune times.

Common Sense Principle #12: Have a real risk case.

I once went to an NBA basketball game with the CFO of a company who was on a nondeal roadshow to see investors. We were having a good conversation about the company while watching the game when he suddenly jumped out of his chair as it appeared that a fan on the other side of him was about to spill beer in his direction. He explained that he would be on the road two more days and that he only brought one pair of pants on the trip. One pair of pants? Are you kidding? Talk about packing light. After thinking some more about it, I suddenly began to worry about the contingency planning at the company I was invested in. Was it similar to the CFO's attitude toward packing? Maybe they did not carry any spare parts at their facilities or have a back-up manager at the plant I wondered. Frankly, I was already concerned about the company regarding other matters and this gave me another reason to be worried.

People are frequently overly optimistic. This idea is detailed in a fabulous book by Tali Sharot titled "*The Optimism Bias – A Tour of the Irrationally Positive Brain*."[10] In the book, Sharot discusses the human tendency to set positive expectations based largely on cherry-picking favorable memories from past experiences. For example, when planning a vacation, parents often focus on only the good times they had during the last trip rather than the kids fighting in the back seat. Or, as with the prior case, the CFO remembers those business trips where he could have got by with only one pair of pants.

Granted, over the course of mankind, it is this prediction of positive outcomes that has been critical in taking the proactive steps for new developments and breakthrough inventions. It encourages risk taking, which is a key pillar of our progression as a society. However, it also often sets unrealistic expectations that can be detrimental in many fields, such as investing.

Instead of taking an overly optimistic view. One must objectively consider the *real* risk cases with their investments. Too often an investor's downside scenario is not the true risk case, as later proven by the price performance in the market. When you initiate a position, you should consider the potential for worst-case scenarios, or at least the impact of very detrimental events on your investment. Even if you think the chances of such occurrences are remote, by doing so, you can develop a contingency plan or a course of action if such a real risk case comes to fruition.

Common Sense Principle #13: Respect the power of debt.

I should probably make a formal apology to any attendees of an "idea dinner" I attended in early 2014. (Idea dinners are small-group events hosted by the sell-side where buy-side PMs and analysts share their best investment ideas.) At the dinner, I presented a trade idea of going long Peabody Energy (the largest U.S. coal producer) and short Joy Global, Inc. (a producer of coal mining equipment). The crux of my thesis was that depressed coal prices would improve well before an uptick in demand for coal mining equipment, given my expectation that the equipment glut around the globe would persist for many years. This thesis sounded good in theory. However, in hindsight, I did not put enough emphasis on the debt levels Peabody was carrying and the stress a further deterioration in both thermal and met coal prices would put on the company's financial viability. Peabody is a large, diverse producer with operations across the major U.S. coal basins as well as in Australia. Also, its debt load was somewhat less precarious than many of its peers (e.g., Walter Energy, Arch Coal, and Alpha Coal), who had also made very high-priced acquisitions in recent years. Still, while my "least stinky pig" theory for Peabody seemed sensible at the time, its financial leverage should have been a bigger concern than I reckoned it to be.

Fortunately, I recognized my failed thesis fairly quickly this time and exited the position before the trade got really ugly. I only hope others at the dinner did the same or didn't follow my recommendation to begin with. I like to think my punting of the trade early on partly related to the lesson I learned from my experience with debt-laden Walter Energy. As proven across much of the coal sector in recent years, things can go downhill quickly for companies with high financial leverage, as large debt levels act as an accelerator leading often to a poor ending. This is particularly when cash flows are negative and when issues like debt covenants or maturities are pressing. Companies in this predicament have been described as "circling the drain," and time generally is not in their favor. This typically is not lost in the marketplace, as the stock price frequently nosedives and begins to reflect a much diminished probability that the company will be able to pull through without having to declare bankruptcy. Needless to say, holding on to a stock going through such a period is very unpleasant.

The financial crisis of 2008/2009 unfortunately led to a number of such scenarios for investors. Nevertheless, I supposed one upside experience from that time was that we equity people suddenly were required to temporarily become debt analysts…or at least to pretend to be debt analysts. This rough period for most companies seemed to increase the equity community's general appreciation for the power of debt and the importance of doing proper due diligence regarding how companies can handle leverage. It also allowed many equity investors to ultimately better position their portfolios for when conditions improved, as conversely the high financial leverage of some companies acted as accelerators to the upside.

Common Sense Principle #14: Know the difference between patience and stubbornness.

This concept was highlighted earlier, but it is so important and violated so often that I want to harp on it again. Successful investors tend to be patient with their ideas, not succumbing to the market fear when a position moves against them yet their thesis remains intact. They critically assess how conditions may have changed and if their reasoning for the trade is no longer valid. But, they hold their ground or even add to the position, if they believe the market is being short-sighted and their thesis will ultimately prevail.

This is far different from stubbornness, which is displayed when investors hold on to a position even though they realize their thesis has been proven wrong or conditions will likely continue to work against them. Stubbornness is a cancer to investment returns. It is the chief cause behind poor slugging, as it commonly leads to large losses in a position that offsets many winners in the portfolio.

Stubbornness is often associated with anger among investors. A PM may be mad that things didn't work out as planned, and now he or she is too upset (and arrogant) to swallow their pride and take the loss. Such investors violate Common Sense Rule #7 and expect to win on every trade.

Stubborn investors pay a large price to Old Man Market. It's acceptable to be upset, but it's not acceptable to let your emotions dictate your actions and prevent you from making rational investment decisions.

Common Sense Principle #15: Get away from negative people.

We all know them. Rainclouds seem to follow over their heads. When you talk to them, you feel the life being sucked out of you, and you start to wonder if the plastic knife in the office kitchen is sharp enough to slash your wrists. These "Debbie Downers" of the office act as if their work is a constant whipping and tend to complain about everything from the company coffee to who didn't deserve their last promotion. My best advice for dealing with these people is simple: STAY AWAY! Fake an incoming phone call, a nose bleed, or a minor stroke. Just somehow remove yourself from conversing with them.

Of course, there are times when we have no choice and have to work with such individuals. In those cases, I believe you must make a conscious effort to stay positive, keep the conversation away from negative topics (if possible), and strive not to let the person's poor attitude infect others in your group. There is already too much negative feedback we receive from the market each day. We don't need additional sources of negativity.

Common Sense Principle #16: Quit Cramming.

I recently was on neighborhood jog on a Sunday morning when it dawned on me that I had to be at our church in 45 minutes. In that time, I needed to cover the 1.5 miles back to our house, shower/dress, feed and dress the kids, review the 6th grade Sunday school lesson (which I was teaching), and get to church. Doable actually…but it was going to be tight and I had better pick up my pace. Unfortunately, as soon as I got home, my wife was in a bit of a panic because she had to leave for an important yoga training class and her car's battery was dead. Going with the only alternative she had at the time, she quickly switched car keys with me and said "good luck." Great. Jump starting the car was not in my 45-minute plan.

In record-book speed, I got a quick jump from a neighbor and somehow got everyone to church on time. (Fortunately, the church is near our house, I take quick showers, and the kids are good with cereal.) The only thing that didn't happen was my reviewing of the Sunday school lesson. Oops…

sorry kids. That week's class probably wasn't the most inspirational to say the least.

Sadly, this fire drill is not that uncommon in our busy household, where everyone has events to attend and commitments to fulfill. Like many families, we have a packed schedule on most days. But our attempt to do it all in a small window of time often seems absurd. Why do we try to cram everything in, leaving no room for delays or anything unexpected? It's foolish. But it doesn't stop at home. At work, how many times have I left for a meeting that is 15 minutes away 15 minutes before the start of the meeting? Or even worse, why do I attempt to send a quick email before I leave with the thought that I can hurry and make it in 12 minutes.

I'm pretty sure I'm not alone in these tendencies. By attempting to squeeze everything into our packed schedules, we create additional noise in our lives and lessen our ability to deliberately and thoughtfully attend to our most important issues. We should resist the pressure of having to fit everything in. Rather, for instance, we should strive to get to the meeting or the event 10 minutes early. Simplifying our schedule and eliminating the rush reduces the chaos surrounding us and provides more clarity in our decisions and actions. We must resist the urge to constantly do more, but instead do what we do better.

Common Sense Principle #17: Don't leverage up personally.

Some may consider the topic of their personal finances off-limits and no one else's business. Even so, this principle is too important not to cover at least briefly and, in my view, it even classifies as common sense. Having a job in the securities sector can be stressful. Thus, I believe it's imprudent to add even more stress, and potentially paint yourself into a corner financially, by leveraging up. Depending on the nature of your firm, compensation in the business can be quite volatile. Sure, you may make a lot of money one year, but you must average it out with other years when perhaps you only receive your base pay. Moreover, as a PM, with the start of every new year, your P&L resets to zero with typically no guarantee what the coming year's payout will be. Then, there is the issue of job security, which is often less in the investment business than with other lines of work.

Given these large unknowns and the potential for your annual cash flows to go through some extreme highs and lows, it makes no sense to me to leverage up personally. Rather, I believe those in the business should use bonuses or whatever additional income they receive to pay down their debts (mortgages, auto debt, student loans, etc.). It makes little difference the attractive interest rate you may have locked in. By maintaining minimal personal debt, you will sleep better at night and be more prepared if your career runs into tough times.

Common Sense Principle #18: It's not a good year until it's over.

Kenny Rogers is right. You shouldn't "count your money when you're sitting at the table." As tempting as it may be, don't change any personal spending habits based on your year-to-date P&L or mid-year review. I know a lot of people that have learned this the hard way. Too many negative things can happen, both to your portfolio or to your firm, which can make your ultimate end-of-year payday well below what you expected. This is another easy one: Don't spend it until it's in the bank.

Common Sense Principle #19: There should be only one gear.

One of my favorite compliments I ever received is when a friend once told me I had only "one gear." I'm not sure he even meant it as a compliment actually (or if I deserved it). But I took it as one anyway. To me, having "only one gear" means that when you go for something, it's either 100% or nothing. Actually, I think that's a good way to lead your life. In whatever endeavor you choose, you should be either all-in, pedal-to-the-metal, full-blast forward or you're out. There really isn't room for anything in the middle. "If it's worth doing, it's worth overdoing," stated Ayn Rand. Life passes by too quickly to short-change yourself and not give full effort in all you do.

Common Sense Principle #20: Learn from the best practices of others.

What's the next best thing to being smart? Having smart friends. Seriously, so much of what I've learned in my career I credit to being around extremely talented, brilliant colleagues and friends. Watching and asking questions of successful people I believe is the best method of learning. Moreover, having a mentor or someone willing to share their experiences and best practices is truly priceless. I also believe it is then our responsibility to be mentors to others and pass down what we have learned. This applies not just to the investment business, but to life in general.

Exhibit 17: Common Sense Principles to Investing

1) Common sense can be contrarian.
2) Risk doesn't have to be so complex.
3) Things change (including companies).
4) Stop dwelling on your losses.
5) Quit thinking the market has to make sense.
6) There is no good or bad luck.
7) Stop expecting to win every day.
8) Don't forget the basics.
9) Don't trust the crowd.
10) Know what you're getting into and have an escape plan.
11) Take only good shots.
12) Have a real risk case.
13) Respect the power of debt.
14) Know the difference between patience and stubbornness.
15) Get away from negative people.
16) Quit cramming.
17) Don't leverage up personally.
18) It's not a good year until it's over.
19) There should be only one gear.
20) Learn from the best practices of others.

Ray: *You mean you never even had a Slinky?*
Egon: *We had part of a Slinky. But I straightened it.*

Movie: Ghostbusters

Chapter 8:

Smart is Fine, But Savviness is Key

One summer morning in my college years when I was back home and staying with some friends at Oklahoma State University, I woke up to an awful sawing sound. I quickly got up from the less-than-comfortable couch I was sleeping on and went to investigate. The noise was coming from the bedroom of a friend who the prior night had complained that his door had swelled such that he could no longer fully close it. When I got to his room, I saw that he was attempting to solve the common problem by climbing onto a desk and leveling off the top of his door with a cheese grater. Ingenious! I guess when you are living in a college apartment with not much more contents than beer cans and pizza boxes, one has to be resourceful. Hence, a cheese grater.

Granted, there are probably better stories to begin a chapter on savviness. Still, as strange as that was, I credit my friend for his creative, albeit bizarre, solution to solving the problem. Although, I'm guessing the landlord did not appreciate this example of out-of-the box thinking.

Early on in the book we discussed specific factors that present opportunities in investing, as well as the process one might follow when researching ideas and managing a portfolio. Next, we explored other important investing topics, namely maintaining a well-founded thesis and understanding the importance of timing. In more recent chapters, we have transitioned to discussing behaviors and characteristics critical for success in the investment business, such as confidence, common sense, and now savviness.

When I first joined the buy-side, I was once arguing the fundamentals of a stock with my boss when he asked me a pointed question, "Do you want to be right, or do you want to make money?" I was fresh from the sell-side where being right, or really just being knowledgeable, was the focus. So I really didn't understand the question. Isn't being correct in your thinking about a company and making money on the stock generally congruent? If I have the fundamentals down pat and know the entity better than most, and then I am proven correct, how can that not be profitable?

Over time, I learned the answer is that being intelligent really isn't enough. In order to consistently make good investments, of course you need to be smart, but some degree of savviness is also required. Just about everyone in the investment business is smart. However, not everyone is savvy.

Through a quick search, one can find several definitions of the word "savviness." The most accurate I believe is: "Acting in manner that is shrewd, well-informed, and perceptive."[1] (All of which are very positive characteristics in investing by the way.) I would also define savviness as "intelligence applied." **Practically speaking, intelligence is often considered theoretical, but savviness is functional**. Savviness gets things done. Savviness finds answers. It is thought of as being more actionable than raw intellect. At times, savviness may involve thinking outside of the box. While in other instances, it's effectively using everything in the box to develop a creative solution or coming up with a less-than-obvious conclusion.

Another definition of savviness that I found is "acting with common sense." I strongly disagree with that description. Like last chapter's topic of common sense, savviness isn't something taught in a classroom or in a textbook. There is no Savviness 101 as far as I know. However, where it differs sharply from common sense is that common sense principles *should* be largely universal, whereas displaying savviness is more unique. Some equate being savvy to being "street smart," which I think somewhat fits the definition. But, it's also more than that. On a broad level, it is portrayed by someone who adeptly understands the various key elements affecting a situation and is able to apply that information to the next level of understanding. It is relevant to situations all around us, not just investing.

In fact, even a recent cookie negotiation between my 6-year old son and myself is a good example of savviness.

"Dad, I want five cookies."
"Five cookies! Five cookies is ridiculous. How about one cookie. It's not long until dinner time."
"Mom lets me have four cookies."
"OK, I know that's not true."
"My sister got three cookies yesterday."
"She did? Well, that's too many. How about two cookies?"
"OK. Two cookies."

Of course I was played. He just wanted two cookies in the first place. In his savviness, he realized that if he started the bidding at five cookies and then brought in other points supporting his case (his mother and sister), I might arrive at a number higher than my normal response of just one cookie. He knew the issue and my likely response before we started our negotiation. So he skillfully crafted his strategy to achieve his desired outcome of two cookies. And Dad fell for it.

Ask Why

My older son also often displayed savviness when he was a young child, but in an unintentional, more curious way. Like many four-year olds, his response to almost everything at that time was "*Why?*".
"Let's go to the park, Son."
"Why?"
"Time to take a bath."
"Why?"
"Pick up you toys."
"Why?"
"Time to go to bed."
"Why?"
It was endless. I know many parents can relate. Understandably, my son's "why's" tended to grow tiresome rather quickly. Nevertheless, as a proud parent, I reasoned that being inquisitive was maybe just a sign that he was intellectually gifted. Questioning the meaning and cause for life's events, and not accepting things at face value, typically requires a higher level of thinking and an eagerness to uncover the less-than-obvious

answers for difficult questions. And of course in my eyes, that was the case with my boy.

OK, maybe I went a little overboard in my ideas of him being nothing short of a child prodigy. But that tends to happen with first children. Regardless, in looking back at it, I believe there is something to be learned from his incessant "why's," particularly as it relates to investing.

Simply asking "why?" is often a good place to start in seeking savviness. For instance, someone may suggest that you buy a stock because it's cheap. Fine, but *why* is it cheap? Are there good reasons for it to be cheap, as well as to remain inexpensive? Is there a catalyst that will possibly alter its cheapness? As discussed previously, are earnings estimates overly aggressive to the point that the stock probably *isn't* cheap after all? Are sell-side analysts drinking management's Kool-Aid? *Why*?

How about buying a company's stock because it has pricing power? But, *why* do they have pricing power? *Why* is it sustainable? Will it invite more competition? Is there a threat from regulators? *Why* isn't it already priced into the stock?

Or, *why* are short interest levels so high for a given stock? *Why* is sentiment so negative? Is it based only on short-term expectations? What factors are giving the shorts conviction or maybe overconfidence? What could they be missing? What could cause them to panic and cover?

Or, on a fundamental level, *why* are margins higher than at a company's peers? Does the corporation have a structural advantage relating to its position in the industry? Do they manage costs better? Are they more efficient? Are there cultural differences that encourage betterment? Is it sustainable? *Why* can't their best practices be copied?

And finally, my favorite "*why*" example: "*Why* in the world is he wearing jeans?" This one takes some explaining. It was a question I once asked a colleague at the BMO global metals and mining conference when the CEO of a large, and very troubled, gold company showed up in jeans at the welcoming cocktail party. Like most participants, he had been to the conference many times and knew that the appropriate attire that evening was slacks and a jacket. I remember then saying to a colleague, "Either he's going to a rodeo after this, or his 'give-a-crap' meter has hit zero and it's another sign of defeat for the company. I'm going to see if I can get a one-on-one meeting with them tomorrow." My colleague later teased me that I made his attire that night the central point of my short thesis for the stock. But, in reality, there were plenty of reasons not to like the company beyond the CEO's inappropriate and unhip blue jeans. Still, I guess noticing that did get me thinking a bit, and asking *"why?"* as it related to several important issues for the company. And that led me to do proper due diligence and ultimately develop a more substantial thesis on the stock.

Other Examples of Applying Savviness in Investing

As it relates to analyzing securities and managing a portfolio, savviness is critical. It comes down to effectively applying your knowledge, making sense out of the noise, looking for an angle, and putting it all together. It's taking your analysis to the next derivative. Often, it means looking at issues not in focus today or critically thinking about what will be important to investors in the future.

Let's think about some other examples. Through your intellect and knowledge of financial analysis and of a particular company, you may conclude that the Street's consensus earnings estimate for the current quarter is too high. However, it is your savviness that might have you analyze the potential timing of an earnings preannouncement and its impact on estimates for next year, which may be more important after the earnings warning has past. For instance, you might check if the company is about to present at a conference or go on a roadshow to see investors. A preannouncement is more likely during those times, since these types of events give management an opportunity to talk about the missed expectations and try to calm any anxious investors. You might also explore if management has made any subtle comments in order to prepare the Street for an earnings miss. You might go back and read the press releases and conference calls with prior disappointments. How did the Street react? Was management forthright or did they seem ambiguous and misleading? How will the Street view this disappointment in light of the other mishaps? Is there now a low bar with the company so that the disappointment might have a minimal impact on the stock price, or are investors more likely to throw in the towel eliciting a sell-off? Are its peers also indicating disappointments? Investigating all these factors is often even more important than concluding the company will likely miss the consensus estimate for the quarter. Your intellect may determine the likelihood of the miss, but your savviness is critical in assessing the timing of the miss, the stock's possible reaction, and other factors that will be important to the Street.

Now let's consider a separate situation where, through your analysis and knowledge, you've concluded a company is a likely takeout candidate. Just being smart may have you stop at that. But being savvy may have you go a step further, such as seeking out which competitors just raised capital or made comments suggesting they might be a potential bidder for the company. Savviness may have you analyze the potential hurdles of various corporate combinations and what price the targeted takeout company would likely require to get a friendly deal done. It may have you explore some of the motivations behind a potential deal...management successorship, regulations, regional tax issues, etc. By analyzing the less-than-obvious issues, you may be able to gain an edge on the probability of a deal actually coming to fruition.

Finally, savvy investors often look for byproducts of an event. Who benefits and who suffers from it? What are the related companies that the Street has yet to consider? Let's return to the down-and-out manufactured housing industry, which appeared to be on its last leg in 2005 when Hurricane Katrina hit the US Gulf Coast. I'm not suggesting emergencies or natural disasters, particularly of this scope, should be unsympathetically viewed as merely investment opportunities. Nevertheless, there were undoubtedly some investors that recognized the coming need for temporary shelter for hurricane victims and identified a short-term opportunity in the depressed manufactured housing stocks, which soared days after the event. Opening up your analytic mind to thinking about how ancillary industries and companies will be affected from an event is a highly-needed, savvy approach that has large benefits to investment returns.

Poor Attempts at Savviness

Being savvy doesn't mean engaging in random, off-the-wall analysis or following a process just because no one else is doing it. I've seen plenty of absurd research and analysis that people claim as savviness, and even call proprietary, but really have no bearing or relevance on a company's stock price or future. On the sell-side, a manager once suggested that in my analysis of the US solid waste industry that I might hire a kid to walk around and count dumpsters in New York City. Seriously? Yes, that would be proprietary, but not very useful. First, NYC is just one of the many markets in the country for the waste haulers. But, even more importantly, what would a random count of containers say about anything? Maybe I could have had the kid count banana peels in the waste bins as well. I couldn't imagine telling a client I had done such pointless analysis.

In another example of a futile attempt at savviness, a Sr. trader at our firm would at times submit a buy order to a floor trader at the exchange with the caveat not to buy shares if another particular trader on the floor was selling. Our trader had overthought his process to the point that he concluded if a certain floor trader was selling (regardless of the amount), then the stock would likely be going lower. This practice thoroughly confused our floor trader who, instead of concentrating on executing the trade at the best price, would have to stop buying once that particular counterparty approached the specialist. When the other trader walked up, the conversations went something like, "Hey, what are you all doing? Are you buyers?" To which the response from our floor trader was, "I'm not sure. That depends on what you're doing." I'm no trader, but I don't think it's supposed to work that way. That's silliness, not savviness.

While this chapter is short, I think its message is immensely important. At investment conferences, there is often talk about who's the "smartest person in the room." While we all hope to be in the running for that title, we should really be seeking to be the "*savviest* person in the room." That's the person who generally is both right and, more importantly, makes money.

Bill the Krill: *"I fear the worst, Will."*
Will the Krill: *"I fear the worst too, but only because fearing the best is an absolute waste of time!"*

Movie: Happy Feet 2

Chapter 9:

Sleeping at Night – Not Overrated

For several years when I was with my prior fund, a trader named Basit in our London office monitored my overseas positions during the sleeping hours in the U.S. (I'm again violating my "no names" policy here. But, since it's a common name in the UK, I think his identity is fairly safe.) Basit is a very good trader and did an excellent job watching my book for me when I was getting shut eye. He would only call me in the middle of the night when there was big news with one of my stocks or when the price of one of my positions had moved a large percentage. Unfortunately, most times he called me it wasn't because of a positive development, and he rarely called to congratulate me on a great idea at 3AM local time. Rather, he normally rang with something negative to report. Hence, I began to unfairly call him "Bad News Basit." In fact, when someone would ask me how I sleep at night during stressful times, I would frequently respond, "I don't. Basit calls me."

A few years ago, one of my larger UK positions had a development that warranted a call to get me out of bed. However, when the phone rang, I thought it was the alarm clock and instinctively reached over to slap the snooze button. Unknowingly, I hit the speaker button on the telephone instead, and suddenly Basit was on speaker in our bedroom quite loudly broadcasting "Hello, Trip. Are you there Trip?" Not having really woken up yet, I thought I was having a dream and Bad News Basit was in it with me. "Just sell it Basit. Just sell it." I was mumbling according to my wife.

I really enjoyed working with Basit, but I must say I don't miss his middle-of-the-night calls or the nightly anxiety of possibly being woken up with news that I would have to act upon. Combined with the normal everyday stress relating to my domestic positions, this led to many nights of tossing and turning and fearing a phone call informing me of a negative development. After several years, I started to analyze my daily anxiety regarding my overseas positions. Did I lack conviction in those names or was it just the thought that I might be woken up at any moment to make a decision affecting millions of dollars while I was still half asleep? How would I ever sleep easily with these positions in my book?

Over the years, I learned to better deal with the anxiety of the PM position and to roll a bit more with the punches. I started to consider the nervousness and stress as necessary evils of the job, as well as even indicators at times that I may be taking on too much risk. I have also sometimes viewed my discomfort as a potential gut feel that I might be on the wrong side of a trade.

In such times of high stress or anxiety, I think it's worthwhile to do a self-assessment of your conviction regarding a position. You should perform a thorough review of your thesis for the trade, your expected outcome, and most importantly the potential risk case. As stated with Common Sense Principle #12, you should ask yourself, "Is my risk case really the true risk case, or am I being too optimistic on the downside to justify holding on to the investment? How realistic is the risk case or even a more severe outlier case? How probable are events that will negatively affect my position?"

Much has been written about probabilistic analysis. It is the practice of assigning probabilities to various scenarios to arrive at an expected outcome for an investment. I have performed such analysis many times and understand the virtues of it. Still, I must admit that I'm fairly cynical on the topic, as I believe it is unreasonable to think that one can accurately and consistently estimate the chances of most scenarios, or especially predict the expected stock price reaction after an event. In reality, such estimates are just guesses often made to fit a predetermined expected outcome. Also, in many instances, probabilistic analysis underestimates the likelihood of the risk case since the person who has done the work is typically biased to deemphasize the downside in order to make a convincing case to initiate or keep the position.

Anxiety in investing often results from holding an aggressive, oversized bet. One story in "*Reminiscences of a Stock Operator*" references a man who can't sleep because he owns too much cotton. The answer from the main character: "sell down to the sleeping point."[1] To review, I believe position size should incorporate the liquidity, volatility, and the expected return of the investment. But it also should be consistent with your gut feel and your stress level of holding on to the position.

Fear of Regret and Hope Trades

One of the reasons investors hold on to losing positions is the fear of regret. The thinking is "If I unwind the position and take a large loss now, I'm not going to be able to live with myself if the trade reverses." The fear of regret seems to increase the longer one has held on to a losing position and as the loss in the position grows. "It's down so much that I might as well hold on to it now" often is the conclusion of many investors.[2]

Unfortunately, at that point, the position has transformed into essentially a "hope trade." The original thesis may be invalid or new developments may have changed the fundamentals for the company, and now you are left merely with hope that the position will revert to its prior levels. It's not a good place to be. Relying on hope trades to work out despite altered fundamentals is obviously a poor investment strategy.

Dealing with the Bad Positions

The summer after my senior year in high school, I wrestled in the Oklahoma All State Games, where wrestlers from the eastern part of the state dueled wrestlers from the western half. The match was in Tulsa on a Friday night. However, it was required of us to arrive on Wednesday to practice with our team. Blackwell is a couple hours from Tulsa, but through various events, I had met and stayed in touch with two separate female acquaintances in Tulsa, both for which I had a strong liking. So, using my 18-year old logic, it made sense to me that one of the nights before the match I would meet up with one girl and the next night I would see the other. (Fortunately, the girls went to separate high schools and did not know each other.) That would have been copacetic, except that I not-so-brilliantly asked them both to come to the match on Friday.

Everything was fine during the warm-ups of the dual. I noticed one girl at one end of the gymnasium and the other on the opposite side. "Great, there will be no problem," I thought. "I just have to figure out how to handle it after the match."

Unfortunately though, sometime during my match, I looked up to where my family was sitting and noticed one of the girls on one side of my parents and the other on the opposite side. "Oh my, now that's a problem," I thought. Thankfully, one of my older sisters recognized the dilemma and somehow defused the situation as well as possible before I finished the match. To this day, I'm not sure how she did it, but I still owe her for that.

This encounter at an early age provided me a notable experience in dealing with a difficult situation. Unfortunately, I've had many others since then, although maybe none as memorable. In fact, I think the most important part of a PM's role is how to effectively deal with bad situations and underperforming positions. When do you cut and run? And when do you size up and capitalize on the Street's misunderstanding?

We previously talked about the need to let go of losing positions once your thesis is no longer valid and before it becomes a hope trade. Still, there are times when you are dealing with a losing position, but have yet to arrive at the likely-needed capitulation point. Unfortunately, during these periods, too much energy and time is often concentrated on the struggling position, which can detract focus from the rest of your book. Simply put, losing trades can suck up your energy and enthusiasm in running a portfolio and can provide for some depressing times.

I was in such a mood one night several years ago around Christmas when my wife and I were in a small bible study group at our church. I had just lost a large amount in one position that day, which had resulted in a sizable hit to my year-to-date P&L. And it had occurred during the most important last few weeks of the year! To say the least, I was not in a joyous holiday spirit and decided I would keep my mouth shut for much of the meeting. Our study started out fairly normal with casual greetings and our leader asking if anyone had any joys or concerns they would like to share. That's when one very nice woman in our group started to describe her stress of preparing for the holidays. What to get everyone? What to do with family coming in town? Where does everyone sit at the dinner table? How long to cook the turkey?...."I'm just '*Christmased*.'" she announced. I almost lost it. *Christmased*?!! Really? That's what you call stress? Could we please change places for a day. I'll cook the turkey and you decipher why one of my positions is getting hit so hard in the market, or how I'm going to make back that money in the last two weeks of the year. In hindsight, I felt terrible thinking that because she is such a nice person. Fortunately, I kept my thoughts to myself and ultimately unwound my losing position shortly after that day, improving my Christmas cheer.

While moving on can be difficult, it's often very healthy for your mental state and your portfolio to put bad trades behind you and tackle new ideas. **I think the main answer to dealing with bad trades is to thoughtfully review the position and your original thesis and try to avoid mentally getting sucked down with the loss.**

Escaping the Noise

In my latest position, when people asked me what I did for a living, I often said "I delete emails...oh, and I run paired equities portfolio on the side." I know many people share my pain. Toward the end of my time at my prior fund, the size of my inbox had become ridiculous. Despite my efforts to "unsubscribe" and be removed from some research distribution lists, the flood of emails I received daily was out of control. I typically had 100 or so emails waiting for me each day when I got to the office, which was mainly research from overseas. Then, another 200-400 emails would come in throughout the day. Sadly, this is pretty typical in the business. Moreover, my email count may have even been low compared to other PMs.

For a long time, I felt compelled to stay on top of it all. I needed to be in touch with my sector and thought that I should know what everyone was saying about the stocks I covered. But, unfortunately, so many of the emails said the same thing or just repeated things that I, and most people following the sector, already knew. That led me to delete most emails at the first glimpse of the title and thankfully finally learning to use the "shift" button for mass deletion.

But, it didn't stop with email. My voicemail was also out of control and so was my Bloomberg messages and chat. Everywhere around me was noise. It was like being in a crowded room with everyone trying to speak to me at once. Again, sadly, I think my experience with this is commonplace with PMs and analysts at sizable funds.

A frequent dilemma I had was deciding if I should ignore the noise completely (a strategy successfully adopted by some PMs) or just surf through emails, voicemails, Bloomberg messages, etc. to find those that seem relevant to my current interest. The latter might keep me more in touch, but it also involves making hundreds of little decisions. Do I keep this email or trash it? Do I want to take a call with that analyst or respond to a salesperson's chat? In aggregate, all those small decisions consumed way too much time in my day, as well as way too much mental energy.

Moreover, the distraction of all this noise hindered me from determining "What do *I* actually think?" Not what was being forced down my throat by others. But what are *my* thoughts and opinions about a particular stock or subject matter?

Over time, I learned the benefit of saying no to meetings, phone calls, and email lists (if possible) and frequently sought out places where I could think without distractions. Sometimes this was in a conference room, during a mid-day walk around the block, or on a plane ride. One of my team members and I even joked that we tended to learn more on the plane ride to a conference than we did at the conference, and that we should just book plane trips around the country when we needed a few hours of undisturbed research.

Unfortunately, the benefits of taking the time to really ponder about what is being said and what is happening and to form your own opinions is getting lost in our world of heightened communication and overabundance of information. Analysts and PMs often feel that they must read every research report and have every small detail in their notes, frequently at the cost of understanding or correctly prioritizing the main impactful issues for a company. I see many junior analysts in company group meetings feverously copying down almost every word management is saying, as if they are a stenographer that is paid by the hour. Obviously, they just want to be able to later relay everything that was said to their boss (the PM or fund owner), who may not seek from them anything beyond the facts. They don't want to be caught not having something in their notes that later on may develop into a big deal. I'm not knocking it. I get the need for CYA (cover your ass) research for analysts in this business. Still, I find it humorous when I look over in a management meeting and notice that a fellow buy-sider has taken half a page of notes although we've barely finished the introductions and the comments about the weather.

In one meeting, a young analyst was busy with his head down banging away notes on his keyboard when he interrupted the CEO after he said a plant was running on three shifts and at 80% capacity utilization. The analyst looked up and asked, "Just to clarify, you are operating at 3% capacity utilization?" Seriously buddy? I know you must have just misheard, but stop typing and think about it for a second. Do you really think a plant would operate at 3% capacity utilization? How about looking up, listening, processing what is being said, and really joining the conversation here.

Many analysts get so lost in the details that they can't put all the pieces together to form a truly insightful question or a real takeaway from a meeting. Instead of taking down every detail of the meeting, what they really should be thinking is, "What is it here that really matters? Is there something no one seems to be grasping? Which topics are getting a lot of attention, but are really trivial to the value of the company? Is management being forthright with us? Is there another angle that I can explore?" Seeking such answers is consistent with the needed savviness discussed in the prior chapter.

In general, taking time to connect with your thoughts and to process the information in your head has huge value. In fact, writing this book has been highly beneficial to me in remembering what I've learned, what I truly think, and the experiences that I've had over the years. What I've realized is there is normally more than enough knowledge and understanding inside of our skulls to make a decision or to have critical insight on a particular subject matter. We just have to tune out the noise and connect with it.

Decompressing

I'll admit it. I get sucked in to watching mindless television sometimes. As my wife can attest, I often have difficulty pulling myself away from some 1980s movie that I've already seen multiple times or a new silly reality show. This happens generally after a long day and when my mind just wants to relax and do nothing (which is helpful in relating to many of the characters on the reality shows). Just like resting other parts of your body after long use, this mental slowdown is healthy and productive…as long as you are able to eventually pull yourself off the couch and join the family for dinner I've learned.

But decompressing doesn't always have to happen at home. It can also be highly beneficial at the office. During stressful times, I've often taken a walk around the block, or the neighborhood if I needed more time, to collect my thoughts and decompress. Or I've gone to visit my kids at school for lunch. Research has shown when the body is under stress, it lessens the brain's cognitive functions and hinders one's ability to process information and make decisions. So why not take a break, regroup, and come back stronger mentally?

On a similar topic, I'm also a big fan of taking a break for a power nap when you are physically exhausted. Rather than struggling through the day, being unproductive, and making bad decisions because of a lack of sleep, taking a quick rest can have significant benefits to both your physical and mental health. It's no surprise that there are gobs of studies supporting this, as well as many examples of unfortunate events that were traced back to sleep deprivation.

It may sound strange, but I've even at times gone down to the parking garage at work and taken a needed 20-minute power nap in my car. In most cases, I've come back much more alert and have had a more productive remainder of the day than I would have otherwise. Obviously, it doesn't have to be a car nap. In fact, some cutting-edge companies have recognized the importance of sleep and designated areas in the workplace for some shut eye. Or you may just have to find a space on your own. Early in my career, I worked with an older gentleman who made it a habit of grabbing a pillow and taking a quick power nap after lunch. He normally did so in a coat closet near our reception area. On several occasions, we would hear a person scream from being startled when hanging up a coat and seeing a body laying on the floor beneath them. That probably didn't make for such a good power nap for him on those days.

Have a Bit of Fun

Maybe my favorite book I've read in recent years is "*Essentialism*" by Greg McKeown. I highly recommend it. I found the book extremely insightful and applicable in identifying ways to empower yourself to accomplish your agenda and to take control of where you spend your time and energy. A considerable amount of the discussion dives deeper into the topics of how to escape the noise and decipher what really matters in our lives.[3]

The book also emphasizes the need to play or have some fun. Many people simply take themselves too seriously, especially in the investment business. I am highly convinced of that. Whereas once in our lives playing and having fun was an integral part of the day, for many employers and worker bees it's generally viewed as slacking off or simply being unproductive.

I'm not talking about creating a workplace environment that is as casual and ineffective as the hit TV show "*The Office*." But having some enjoyment, be it kidding around with a co-worker or playing a game of paper toss at the receptacle, can serve as a healthy break and a distraction from stress. A friend of mine runs an institutional equity sales and trading branch office for a major investment bank. When moving into a new space, he insisted that they make room on the trading floor for a ping pong table that can be wheeled in and out for use after the market close. "Everyone loves it. We've had some great matches," he says. Unquestionably, making that simple effort to give people a break in their day for some fun has boosted morale and enhanced the overall work environment for his staff.

Many years ago as an associate research analyst, my colleagues and I seemed to have no problem in creating our own fun at the office. Maybe it was just that we weren't making enough money to take ourselves too seriously. Still, we worked hard and fulfilled our responsibilities. We also found time to have contests like the "clip game." In short, the rules of the clip game were that players (clippers) must clip the clothing of another member of the office (clipees) with a plastic binder clip without the person noticing. Then, the attached clip must be witnessed by another participant in the game. The larger the clip, the more points that were awarded. Also, more points were given for clipees that were higher up in the organization.

The most notable moment of the clip game involved a short fellow research associate and friend of mine who was a very talented clipper. One day, our firm's head of trading came marching through the research department looking for a particular analyst. He was a big man with bulldog-like features and was always very intense. As he rummaged around, from my cubical I could see in the corner of my eye my vertically-challenged friend sneak up behind him and clip his jacket with a big 50-point clip. Bravo! I'm quite certain it was the funniest, as well as the bravest, act I've witnessed in my career. The head of trading unknowingly wore the clip for much of the day and we automatically declared my friend the winner of the clip game. (By the way, my friend is now an accomplished analyst that often appears on CNBC and will probably never admit taking part in the clip game.)

Another creative contest was called the "meow game." That was seeing how many times you could get away with saying (under your breath) the word "meow" in a meeting. For instance, in a meeting with management of a company you might say, "I wanted to ask you about your capital expenditure plans…(clear your throat)..*meow* What figure are you budgeting this year?" It was important to meow quickly and keep talking.

Fortunately, rarely did people not aware of the game catch it. But it was always quite hilarious to others in the meeting who were in the contest.

OK, maybe the clip and meow games are a bit too childlike for most work environments. Nevertheless, my point is that somehow we should reconnect with those times when we had fun with our profession and enjoyed those around us, rather than taking ourselves so seriously all the time. That's not slacking off. It's being smart about our mental wellbeing and becoming a more cordial and effective employee for your company.

Just Breathe

In addition to being one of my favorite Pearl Jam singles, the title of this segment signifies something I've recently learned and applied in my life because of yoga. Let me offer some background. In 2012, my wife (with my help behind the scenes) opened a yoga studio in Dallas called *We Yogis®*, with the intention of creating a non-intimidating yoga community focused on a tagline of "*Yoga for All.*" The idea started when my wife suggested early that summer that we begin offering free yoga classes in the garage of our home. I thought she had gone mad. "That's disgusting. There are grease pools in our garage that are older than the kids. Besides, what do we know about yoga?" I said. Nevertheless, she convinced me that one of our neighbors had just become certified in the practice and that it was a low-risk way to explore starting a business. I had done yoga through DVDs in the P90X exercise program, which seemed pretty good, and my wife practiced fairly regularly. Plus, we needed to clean the garage anyway. So why not?

A few months later after hosting many packed sessions in the garage, we found an attractive location for a studio, and our garage classes turned into an actual business, which we have now grown to three Dallas locations. A key to our success has been a focus on bridging the often seemingly large gap between traditional fitness and yoga, and thus catering more to the mainstream fitness seeker than is the case with most yoga studios. We've accomplished this largely by favoring the athletic aspects of yoga. In particular, our most popular and challenging class is called Rockin Yogis™, which is a very active vinyasa flow set to upbeat, hip music. It is a terrific workout and a large departure from the common preconception of yoga. Even after a strenuous class, clients leave our studios feeling rejuvenated and with a sense of accomplishment.

Personally, yoga has helped me regain much of my long-lost flexibility that came with wrestling. It is also very effective in providing other physical benefits such as core strength, better posture, weight loss, muscle building, improved overall appearance, and enhanced general athleticism. (Just see how much farther you will hit the golf ball or how much harder you will strike the tennis ball after adding a little yoga in your life.) Therefore, after this promotional diatribe, it goes without saying that I'm big believer in the physical benefits of yoga and would encourage any non-yogis reading this to try it out.

I am also a big believer in the mental wellbeing that yoga promotes. In particular, I have found the practice to be highly effective in releasing anxieties, shutting out the outside world, and reconnecting with my thoughts. Actually, some of my best investment revelations have occurred on the yoga mat. (Even though that may not have been the intention of the class.) Of course, my positive experience with yoga is not unique. The practice has become an important part of life for many accomplished individuals across our society from athletes to business men and women to school teachers. In fact, Inc. magazine listed yoga in a recent article titled, "30 CEOs Reveal the Daily Habits Responsible for Their Success."[4]

Yoga has also taught me the importance of breath. When encountering challenging postures or when feeling fatigued, our instructors frequently remind clients to focus on their breath and try to breathe through any discomfort. It's a very effective tactic, and undoubtedly why breathing for women is such a crucial part in helping to get through the pains of childbirth. Looking back, I wish I had focused more on breath in my wrestling years, since nervousness and ineffective breathing during competition was frequently a problem for me in big matches.

However, such an emphasis on breath isn't something that is helpful only on the yoga mat or in athletic competition. I highly recommend trying it during stressful times or even throughout the workday. It doesn't take much effort. During anxious times, remembering to take a break for perhaps ten long breaths (preferably not while staring at your computer screen or talking on the phone) can have very calming and restorative effect on your body and possibly enable you to better approach your current situation. If you want to spend more time and take it to a higher level of mediation, that's great and all power to you. But, at a minimum, just take some time to breathe.

"Looks like you've been missing a lot of work lately."
"I wouldn't say I've been missing it, Bob"

Movie: Office Space

Chapter 10:

Burnout and Keeping Perspective

Several years ago, I attended a conference in Florida and shared a cab back to the airport with a PM from a Canadian pension plan, who seemed to fit the definition of a long-term investor. He came across as a smart guy, very thoughtful about how he approached stocks, and pretty stress-free. In our conversation, he said, "Oh, you work for a hedge fund. So do you have to check stock prices like multiple times a day?"

"Ummm....Well, yeah, even multiple times an hour many days...or almost constantly on really volatile days." I said.

"Wow...That's intense." he replied.

"Yes, it can be. Why? How often do you look at your screen?"

"Oh, not very frequently. Sometimes I can go days without looking at a stock price."

What? I couldn't imagine that and I thought to myself, "How does this guy have a pulse? Is he the reason they still print pages of closing stock prices in the *Wall Street Journal*?"

I initially thought this guy's work sounded like the ultimate boredom. I wondered how one could get out of bed and do that job every day. Didn't he need a little more action or sense of competition in his life? But just a few weeks later, during a frustrating short-term drawdown in my book, I better understood the appeal of his job and was even a bit envious of his luxury of not being constantly stressed about his positions and the volatility of his portfolio.

Ironically, that conversation happened around the same time as my annual physical, where my doctor said to me, "Yeah, I've got four of you stock market guys as patients. You're the oldest one. Stressful job. You know, you should probably quit doing that after a while." Oh, thanks a lot Doc. I assume I can count on you to start sending checks to my house at that time?

Of course, I had no plans to follow the doctor's advice. Despite his comments on my age, I was only approaching what is generally considered the prime of one's career. Nevertheless, he did have a point. The stress of the job and the emotional ups and downs can take a toll. As highlighted earlier, the constantly-quoted market makes success or failure really too quantifiable, especially on a daily basis. As a PM, every moment on the job you can answer the question of "How's your day going?" with a number. (My wife has frequently reminded me that a "fine" or "very well thank you" response is really what the other person is looking for.) And when you're not at work, you're always thinking about your portfolio. In the past, people have asked me how many hours a week do I work. I've said it depends. Do I count only those hours at the office or on my laptop? Or do I also count the time when I'm pushing one of my kids on the swing set and pondering if a particular company is going to beat its guidance in the upcoming quarter? Does lost sleep count? If so, I may have investment banker hours after all.

Like other intense activities, one's enthusiasm for the job can go through some highs and lows. After many years, the trades can begin to blur and the good months kind of blend in with the bad (as long as the bad aren't really that bad). After experiencing many of the ups and downs you may finally gain some perspective and begin to ask yourself, "Why am I getting this upset if I know the pain is temporary and I'm just having a bad run or a bad day?" Unfortunately though, the pressures of the job are not just from within. It's not a hard concept to grasp that at most firms when you are doing well, you don't get much attention from management above, but you certainly do when you're dragging down the overall performance of the fund.

It's not that PMs or analysts lose the drive to make money. But, it should be no surprise that the large amount of energy and perseverance required to compete in this business each day can foster burnout, especially after doing it for a long period continuously. I've even thought of it as a long stint at the blackjack table. Your chip stack goes up and down, and your emotions follow. You've experienced some fun and exciting at times. But now it's 3am. You've had a good number of drinks, the noise from the slots is finally getting annoying, and there's virtually no one left in the casino except you and a woman smoking a cigarette at your table. By now, you're just going through the motions…"hit me"…"stay"…"hit me"…. Someone just needs to tell you to call it a night and go to your room and go to bed.

Some of my friends have asked how burnout is possible with a job that can be so lucrative. All you need is a few good years, right? Why not just keep playing?

I know some in the business may have a problem with the prior gambling analogy. But, I would contest that even though we place bets we feel are very educated, they are still bets. Someone enviably wins and someone loses, even if it's losing by way of exiting a position too early or keeping it too long. And while the analysis required of an investment seems very different from gambling, trying to predict the short-term performance of a market-driven security at times can be more similar to wagering than investing, regardless of the amount of work behind the idea. Moreover, with a greater number of short term-conscientious players involved today, that unpredictability has been significantly amplified. Behavioral influences and crowdedness often temporarily trump the primary fundamental factors (earnings, cash generation, return on capital, etc.) that determine the value of a security over the long run.

Granted, a shorter-term orientation among market participants has been the trend for many years now. It's not new news that today the vast majority of the trading volume (setting aside high frequency trading) and price gyrations can be attributed to the activity of hedge funds, rather than the mutual fund giants that dominated trading in decades past. In most cases, their short-term point of view is inevitable because their investors didn't sign up for a 2/20 model (the hedge fund industry standard of 2% fees on principle and 20% on profits) to lose money, either in the short, medium, or long-term.

I would argue though in today's post-financial crisis world, most everyone is skittish to a certain degree and has to pay at least some attention to short-term performance. That even goes for most of the long-only funds who may claim to be 100% long-term focused, but in all honesty realize it only takes one year of significantly underperforming their benchmark to reverse money flows and significantly shrink the size of their fund.

Finally, Wall Street research over the past decade or two has also gravitated to placing a greater priority on writing shorter-term ideas and updates and taking a more near-sighted view in general. This naturally caters to the hedge fund community, who, since they largely dominate trading activity, as a consequence account for the major portion of broker commissions. Gone are the days where research was largely focused on appeasing corporate management and generating investment banking revenues. That came to an end thanks to the post-dot-com boom/bust regulations that required enhanced firewalls between the capital markets and investment banking divisions within the banks. The research reports prior to that time typically had more fluff to please corporate clients, but they also often took a bigger picture approach to evaluating and discussing a company. These days, even seasoned sell-side analysts must spend much of their time writing notes with near-term expiration dates and responding to a deluge of calls from their buy-side counterparts about their thoughts on short-term issues, like a company's upcoming quarterly results.

The crowdedness of the short-term game can naturally make a PM's life quite frustrating at times. With many trades, there are simply too many people chasing the same carrot. Several years ago, I played golf with a PM at another large market-neutral hedge fund who covered primarily the same stocks as me. By the end of the round, we talked about almost the entire sector and determined our portfolios were nearly identical. Great minds think alike, right?

Another friend of mine who is a PM at a large multi-manager hedge fund platform told me his company has eleven pods that invest in the same sector as his focus. That's eleven groups with the exact same strategy, trading in the exact same stocks, and often coming up with the exact same ideas. Moreover, they are competing against each other in the 100-meter dash of investment survival, since the underperforming teams generally get eliminated. Now that may be an extreme example, but it does highlight the heightened level of short-term competition in the market today. Whereas the competition used to have various time lines and risk parameters, today most of the major influencers of stock prices are playing the same game.

This is not to say long-term or consistent success in a short-term focused investment world is unachievable or even that rare. Of course, there are many talented and successful PMs who have not only survived, but have thrived in their job for years. If viewed as a round of golf, it's not that they've made all pars and birdies in their career. Yes, they've had their share. But, more importantly, they've tended to avoid the blow-up holes and have lived to play on. They also probably have a good sense of evaluating risk, knowing when to try to hit it over the water and when to lay-up. Finally, they likely maintain the correct perspective of not expecting to win every day (see Common Sense Principle 7 in Chapter 7), as well as the savviness that avoids overcrowded situations and identifies key points not currently in focus by most of the Street.

Still, such perspective, composure, and consistent approach can be difficult to attain for other PMs. It's easy to get energized when you just made a great trade or after you've cashed in on a good year. However, most PMs will tell you the emotional lows are lower than the highs are high. And when you find yourself back in the lows, which seemed so inconceivable after you were recently on the top of the world, the common anxious feeling of "How do I turn this around?" is constantly on your mind. The toughest part of the job is gritting it through those times and getting to the brighter days.

Granted, I'm probably painting an overly bleak portrait of the portfolio manager or analyst job. It's well known that such positions are highly coveted given their fast-paced, intellectually-demanding, and lucrative nature at most firms. I have relished working in such an environment most of the time. As a former athlete, I love the competition, the hard work required, and even the constant scoreboard. Similarly, most of the people I know and have worked with in the business are drawn to the job for those reasons as well. Still, such intensity and volatility can lead to burnout and frustration even with the most aspiring, talented, and committed individuals.

Staying Motivated and Keeping Perspective

So how do you keep the fire going? How do you maintain perspective during the tough times? The answers to these questions differ for each person. I can only say what has helped keep me going and pressing on, especially when conditions are frustrating or the prospects for making money seem grim.

- **Take it one day at a time, one investment at a time.** Probably the most frustrating and depressed period of my wrestling career was my sophomore year at Cornell. It was a cold, snowy January day in Upstate New York. I was thoroughly depressed. I was wrestling terribly and had lost my starting position on the team. The other students were just coming back to school from winter break, while our team had already been there three weeks training. My non-wrestling friends were busy attending parties and eating and drinking significant quantities. Conversely, I was attending two or three workouts a day and eating scraps to keep my weight low.

For the first time, I began to wonder if all the sacrifice was really worth it. I was envious of the good times my non-wrestling buddies were having and I couldn't see how I was going to emerge from the rut I was in. I was walking through the campus to the wrestling office to tell the coach I had had enough. But somewhere along the way, I decided I simply wouldn't think about everything and would just put my head down and get through the day. I used that strategy the next day and then the next and the next…until my attitude began to improve and my wrestling did as well.

Fortunately, this strategy of taking it one day at a time was not only useful in wrestling. It has been highly applicable in my working career, as well as during other difficult times in life. As for investing, when things are not going your way, it's important to take it one trade and one day at a time. Concentrate on what's in front of you and don't be overwhelmed by the forces that seem at play against you. Keep the perspective that each day is a new day.

➢ **Take breaks.** As I write this, I'm fortunate to be on a short hiatus from my career in the investment business. The idea of taking such a pause was nerve-racking to me initially. How was I going to stay in the information flow and keep my edge? The reality is that taking a break from the noise has been tremendously therapeutic, especially in collecting my thoughts and recharging my batteries. It's a great cure for the burnout discussed earlier in this chapter. Too often, PMs or analysts think they need to seek out a new profession because they are burned-out. Rather, what they likely need is simply a break to reconnect with their thinking and reenergize their passion for the business.

I understand that taking such a sabbatical from the job isn't a reality for many people. Nevertheless, I believe it's important to take temporary breaks, such as vacations or long-weekends, and to truly decompress. Turn off your mobile phone and don't check your email. Make a valiant effort to escape the noise and chaos of your job. By not worrying about your productivity or all you have to do, you can return to work with much more vigor than if you had made a half-hearted attempt to break away.

By the way, taking a break generally has to be a proactive endeavor. No one at your job is likely going to tell you to work less. On the sell-side, our director of research once wrote an email to the analysts at the end of summer welcoming them back from any vacations and telling everyone it was now time to hunker down and get to work. Wait a second. I must have missed the email saying to relax and take it easy. The analysts who didn't wait for such a message obviously benefited by coming back more rejuvenated than those who viewed such time off as unnecessary.

➢ **Capitalize on small victories.** This was discussed previously. Still, I want to reiterate again the benefit of turning the tide and changing your momentum through building on small victories. Use small wins to energize you, boost your confidence level, and set a new course.

➢ **Focus on what's most important to you.** My portfolio was having a terrible time around the birth of our third child in September 2009. I had made strong profits early in the year, but those were being rapidly wiped away. Nevertheless, I found perspective very quickly when my son was born early with premature lungs and had to spend two weeks in the NICU at the hospital before coming home. For a few days early on, it was quite dicey. We were busy praying for the health of our new baby, and my recent portfolio loses couldn't have seemed more irrelevant. During my son's time at the hospital, I was probably most in touch with what was truly important in my life. My portfolio took some time to turn around, but I was relatively calm regarding my P&L, as I had a more important focus at that time. Fortunately, my son came out of that period healthy and in flying colors. Now, at six years old, he's still our baby, but also my tough boy that likes to mix it up with his older brother and sister. He serves as a reminder to me of that time and the perspective I need to maintain of what's most important in my life.

- **Realize difficulties are temporary.** In yoga, savasana is the quiet meditative period at the end of class when you relax, lay on your back, and let your thoughts go. In one recent class, the teacher told us to picture yourself in a car on a straight highway. With you in the car are those people in your life most important to you. Then, the teacher asked us to picture life's events as passing cars in the opposite direction that are quickly forgotten once they are by you. Think of the difficult times and tough circumstances as fleeting moments that are pressing today but gone tomorrow. Personally, I also like to think of the car driving to a brighter and better place on the horizon, which for me brings in a religious meaning.

Everyone encounters difficult times with their job or other parts of their life. With investing, I believe the key to having a successful, long-term career in the market is keeping this perspective. The tough times are temporary and we must drive on to brighter days and strive to be the best we can be.

Appendix

Scenario Analysis

I thought it would be beneficial to walk through ten common scenarios that PMs encounter, which present the opportunity to engage some of the practices discussed in this book. Of course, these represent just a small sampling of the many investment scenarios, for which the appropriate response differs significantly by the particular circumstance of each investment. In many of these cases, there is no correct answer, or the correct action is only clear in hindsight. The main point here is to consider how to best respond to the various scenarios and potentially difficult decisions that one is commonly faced with when investing in stocks or managing a portfolio.

Scenario 1 – Earnings Miss by Industry Favorite

The situation: A stock you own is an industry favorite. It has a strong track record, a good balance sheet, management is viewed favorably by the Street, and it's well positioned in its sector. Uncharacteristically, due to higher-than-expected operating costs, the company has missed the consensus earnings estimate for the quarter and has similarly reduced its annual earnings guidance. The higher costs involve the corporation's primary division, but are given an adequate and thorough explanation in the company's press release. When the market opens, the stock immediately drops 5% (approximately a 1.5x daily standard deviation move).

Your move: We are starting with a scenario where best reaction is fairly obvious in most cases. Sell-offs in industry favorites due to one-time misses generally do not last long, particularly if the core fundamentals of the business have not changed. Given that management has strong investor approval and if it indicates the troubles are temporary or fixable, it's probable that the Street will give the company a pass this time and investors will view the price decline as a "buying opportunity" (likely an appropriate use of the term in this case). As always, you should consider factors such as the front-page holders of the stock and if shorter-term funds have reason to get antsy with their positions. But, assuming that your thesis has not changed with the miss, you should probably use the price decline as quick, opportunistic chance to add to your position at a discount.

Scenario 2 – Another Earnings Miss (reasonable stock decline)

The situation: A stock you own has incurred another earnings miss and management has also lowered its annual guidance again. The stock represents a contrarian position for you, as you previously thought the company was on the mend. However, with another disappointment, your thesis for a near-term turnaround is in jeopardy. Still, the case for it being a cheap stock relative to its peers remains, as the 5% decline in the annual earnings guidance equals the stock's price decline on the day of the miss, resulting in an unchanged earnings multiple.

Your move: In this case, your reaction may be dependent on the patience you are willing, or able, to have with the contrarian position. Nevertheless, with your original thesis in jeopardy, there is now a high risk of thesis creep (creating an alternative thesis to justify holding on to the position). The stock may still look inexpensive to peers, but it is difficult to argue for multiple expansion in the face of yet another disappointment. In fact, multiple compression in the valuation may be more likely now. Moreover, potential new investors may avoid the stock and conclude it is a "value trap." (See Alcoa example in Chapter 2.) While selling the position when it is down 5% is not ideal, it still may be the correct decision as there is little reason for it to bounce back to its prior level (implying a multiple expansion). It is important to identify this as a potential "hope trade" if the fundamentals do not support your original thesis.

Scenario 3 - Another Earnings Miss (large stock decline)

The situation: Same situation as Scenario 2, but this time the stock is down 10% on the day of the miss (approximately a 3x daily standard deviation move for the security).

Your move: This one is more difficult. The company's disappointing performance is undoubtedly being reflected to a large extent in the price decline. It may even be considered an overreaction by some investors and analysts, particularly as the stock's valuation has fallen. (Its earnings multiple has declined since its stock price has fallen more than the expected drop in earnings). Still, your thesis is no longer valid and doesn't support holding on to the position. So do you capitulate now and lock-in the loss with the stock down such a large percentage, or hope that the 10% decline is partly an overreaction and that you'll be able to get out of the trade at a better price (maybe similar to Scenario 2)? On one hand, the initial 10% fall may be a precursor to a further decline later in the day (perhaps after the company's conference call) or later in the week (possibly after reactionary downgrades by sell-side analysts). This would make selling at current levels appear less deplorable. Alternatively, reassuring comments by management on the conference call or buying by value investors could lead to some rebound in the stock. Again, the correct decision (if there is one) varies substantially with each circumstance. There are many other variables that need to be considered, such as crowdedness (Did many of your peers have a similar contrarian point of view, which may add further selling pressure?), short interest levels (Will covering by the shorts help support the price?), frustration by longer-term shareholders (Will they finally throw in the towel?), or actions by management (Can they convince the Street things are not that bad?). Personally, in such a situation, if I feared an even larger sell-off, I would be biased to unload at least some shares, leaving the potential to unwind more of the position if the share price improved. On the positive side, this at least somewhat mitigates the total loss if the negative price momentum continues, as well as still leaves you with a substantial position if the price rallies. Patient investors may disagree with this strategy, arguing to hold on or even add to what they view as an oversold security. However, this could be imprudent given your failed original thesis. Again, there is generally not an easy answer to this one.

Scenario 4 - Positive earnings surprise (stock surging)

The situation: A stock you own has reported a positive earnings surprise and management has raised its annual guidance. Reasons for the earnings beat are consistent with your thesis for the position and have positive implications for results in upcoming periods. The stock opens up 10% on the day of the earnings beat (approximately a 3x daily standard deviation move).

Your move: You nailed this one. The question now is do you take some profits or keep your full position given the positive momentum with the company and the stock price? Much of this decision should rest on your target prices for your base and best case scenarios. With the latest positive development, you may now be aiming for your best case target price, or maybe the results were good enough to justify bumping up your targets all together. Still, in most instances of large price moves, my inclination is to take at least some of the trade off the table, especially if the position is now relatively close to my original base case target. Of course, we want to let our winners run and not unwind too much if the momentum is expected to continue. Nevertheless, booking some profits on large one-day moves is often a prudent decision, particularly as profit taking by other shareholders may ultimately result in a less extended short-term price move.

Scenario 5 - Positive earnings surprise (small reaction in stock)

The situation: Same situation as Scenario 4, but this time the stock is trading close to flat on the day.

Your move: I hate this one. You were right on the fundamentals, but are not getting paid for it. As discussed in Chapters 1 and 3, you must assess if your thesis was simply part of consensus and thus expectations were higher than you had thought going into the event, or if there are factors that are just temporally muting the share price reaction, such as a macro issue impacting the entire market. If the better-than-expected earnings and guidance was the main factor to your thesis, it is probably worthwhile to consider if you still have a valid reason to hold on to the position. I'm not saying you should abandon all patience with the trade, especially if things are going well for the company. But, you also shouldn't have a thesis-less position in your book either (see Chapter 4). In most cases, my initial preference here is to hold on to such positions, to closely monitor sentiment and any issues that may discredit the original thesis, and to add to the position if it appears that temporary or extraneous issues are the main reason for the subdued share price reaction.

Scenario 6 - Ratings downgrade (large stock decline)

The situation: A stock you own is down substantially due to a ratings downgrade by a well-known sell-side research analyst.

Your move: The appropriate response here likely relates to the nature of the downgrade. Is it based on a proprietary uncovering or an issue that is new to the Street? Will it help change sentiment or possibly be followed by similar downgrades? Alternatively, does it merely reflect the analyst giving up on the stock or updating his or her model and price target based on well-known factors? An example of the latter is a downgrade of a gold producer based on a lower assumed gold price after prices have already fallen. In downgrades where a new fundamental issue is introduced, it's naturally more probable that the share price response is appropriate, and therefore you should closely assess how the issue impacts your thesis. Conversely, I am often surprised at large price moves following ratings changes that are based on already well-known issues or on macro assumptions. In some of these cases, the analyst's reputation or the size of his or her firm holds enough weight to move the stock to an exaggerated level, especially if it's a smaller, less-followed company. In those cases, where new information is not present, increasingly your position is frequently a profitable move.

Scenario 7 - Didn't get the trade on (stock surging)

The situation: A stock is surging on a development that you correctly anticipated or that you view as major positive. Unfortunately, you do not have an ownership position in the company. You might have just got the timing wrong, or you may have wanted to avoid an event risk relating to another issue.

Your move: Do you chase the stock and buy it after it has jumped? With the positive development, you may now be able to justify a much higher price target, making the stock still appear attractive even after the large move. In general, as discussed in Chapter 6, my inclination is not to chase large daily price moves, even when the news appears to be a game-changer. Despite possibly knowing the subject matter better than most investors and being aware of the potential for the development beforehand, you generally do not have any edge at that point. The catalyst has occurred and is largely being reflected in the share price already. Jumping on the bandwagon at the much higher price does not appear to be a particularly savvy move, and could be a costly one if the stock gives up some of its gains because of profit-taking by existing shareholders. Rather, I generally prefer to wait in these cases and see if the market gives me another chance to act upon my positive view at lower price levels.

Scenario 8 – Actions by activist shareholder (stock you are short is surging)

The situation: A stock you are short is up a large percentage because an activist has taken (or is rumored to take) a stake in the company.

Your move: This has become a more common scenario in recent years given the greater frequency of activist positions being taken. The difficult aspect of this scenario is that often the initial reason for your short position (the negative factor for the company) is the same reason motivating the activist. Thus, what was once a negative for the company has suddenly become a positive opportunity for change in the eyes of the market. Additionally, the presence of the activist may significantly improve the Street's overall sentiment toward the stock and create a theoretical floor in the share price (often at the level where the activist fund acquired the majority of its position). These factors may be ample reasons to rethink your short position. Alternatively, the activist's demands may be farfetched, or it may be unlikely that the activist will be able to win enough seats to gain control of the company's board of directors. In that case, the large move in the stock could be unjustified and present the opportunity to increase your short position.

Scenario 9 – Death by a thousand cuts (stock trending against you)

The situation: A contrarian position in your portfolio falls by a small amount each day, but in aggregate represents a large decline from your entry point. Data points have yet to support your contrarian stance.

Your move: Such a scenario relates to the Chapter 5 discussion on timing and opposing momentum. In this case, you may be simply too early in calling an inflection point. It's probably worthwhile to review your thesis and particularly the catalysts that may be needed to reverse the momentum. Again, being too early on a trade can be the same as being wrong if you dig yourself too large of a hole while waiting for the position to turn around. Remember to be very careful regarding position size when opposing momentum.

Scenario 10 – Portfolio getting hit on macro issues

The situation: Your portfolio seems to be disproportionately hit on days when commodity prices fall or when emerging markets decline.

Your move: This is likely a concentration issue. As discussed in Chapter 3, you may be making the common portfolio mistake of having the same theme shared across your portfolio, even if your positions are in different sectors. For example, an oilfield services company and a Canadian bank may seem unrelated in what they do, but their connection to commodity prices is often the same overriding factor to the performance of both stocks. When you recognize positions in your portfolio are moving in tandem, you should closely review the major macro issues impacting each position and determine the level of correlation across your positions, as well as possible unintended bets your portfolio as a whole may represent.

Acknowledgements

I wrote this book for me. (How's that for a start in listing my appreciations?) I wrote it to connect with the muddled thoughts in my head, to sort out the noise, to remember the lessons I've learned, to reflect on the interesting times, to reminisce on the humorous stories, and to prepare for what's next. I began writing it one night when I was faced with the choice of starting a new Netflix series or attempting to get some of my thoughts and stories on paper before I forget them. In doing so, I do not think I solved any of life's mysteries. But, the process has been mentally rewarding and even therapeutic in some ways. It's also been a lot of fun. So I would encourage others to do the same. Even if you don't think you have much to write about, you might be surprised how much is in your head when you tune out the noise.

I first want to thank those who have provided me endless support, and who encouraged me to write this and to share it with others. The top of that list is my beautiful wife and three wonderful children, for whom I am so truly blessed. Also, I would like to thank my parents, in-laws, and siblings for their constant love and encouragement (in particular my father, sister, and a few close pals, who suffered through reading some very rough drafts of this). Next, I'm extremely appreciative of my numerous friends and colleagues that I've come to know over the years in the business and who have helped me attain the knowledge to write this, as well as played key roles in many of the comical stories I've included. My "no-names" policy for this book is saving a lot of space here, since otherwise I could include quite a long list of people that have positively influenced my life and for which I am very grateful.

Finally, I want to thank the sport of wrestling and the people that coached, encouraged, and motivated me during that influential period of my life. Not that I had extraordinary accomplishments in the sport, but what I got from it was far more valuable than a winning record. Fortunately for me and many others, the virtues learned from wrestling are highly transferable to other parts of life, one being a job in the securities business. And so, even after over two decades removed from competition, wrestling continues to shape who I am today. Undoubtedly, it will remain a major influence on how I will live my life going forward. In my mind, there is no greater sport.

NOTES

Introduction

1. Edwin Lefevre, *Reminiscences of a Stock Operator* (Hoboken, New Jersey: John Wiley & Sons, 2006; Originally published: New York: George H. Doran and Company, 1923)
2. Randy Pausch in *The Last Lecture;* http://www.goodreads.com/work/quotes/3364076-the-last-lecture

Chapter 1

1. Illusory Superiority: http://www.urbandictionary.com/define.php?term=Illusory%20superiority
2. Illusory Superiority: https://en.wikipedia.org/wiki/Illusory_superiority
3. Nassim Nicholas Taleb, *Fooled by Randomness* (New York: TEXERE, part of the Thomson Corporation, 2004)
4. Super Bowl theory and results: http://espn.go.com/nfl/superbowl/history/winners
5. Super Bowl theory and results: http://www.1stock1.com/1stock1_141.htm
6. www.clevelandresearch.com
7. Regulation FD definition - Fast Answers (www.sec.gov/answers)

Chapter 2

1. OSK 2Q 2014 news release: http://phx.corporate-ir.net/phoenix.zhtml?c=93403&p=irol-newsArticle&ID=1952280
2. *Cognitive Dissidence:* https://en.wikipedia.org/wiki/Cognitive_dissonance
3. *Cognitive Dissidence:* http://www.simplypsychology.org/cognitive-dissonance.html
4. Contrarian definition: http://www.webster-dictionary.net/
5. Sell-side analyst coverage: Bloomberg
6. Variant Perception: What's Your Variant Perception? Stephen Ellis, March 9, 2006. http://www.fool.com/investing/value/2006/03/09/whats-your-variant-perception.aspx
7. Variant Perception: http://www.variantperception.com/
8. Ichan-Ackman interview: http://video.cnbc.com/gallery/?video=3000143591
9. Agnico-Eagle reeling from Nunavut mine fire - CBC News Posted: Mar 29, 2011 5:17; http://www.cbc.ca/news/canada/north/agnico-eagle-reeling-from-nunavut-mine-fire-1.1044305
10. Elvis Paradox: http://www.murderousmaths.co.uk/elvis.htm
11. "Warren Buffet Explains Why Fear Overshadows Greed" - CNBC: Aug 11, 2011, 2:20 pm EST; http://www.cnbc.com/id/44108052
12. "Ebola Spread in Dallas Elevates Public Fear" - Houston Chronicle: Oct 13, 2014; http://www.houstonchronicle.com/news/houston-texas/houston/article/Ebola-spread-in-Dallas-elevates-public-fears-5818573.php
13. "Eli on Ebola: 'I think we'll be fine'" - ESPN: Oct 16, 2014; http://www.espn.com/new-york/nfl/story/_/id/11707088/new-york-giants-brief-players-ebola-virus-ahead-trip-dallas

Chapter 3

1. Sharp ratio: http://www.investopedia.com/terms/s/sharperatio.asp
2. Endowment Effect: http://endowment-effect.behaviouralfinance.net/
3. Endowment Effect: http://www.investopedia.com/terms/e/endowment-effect.asp

Chapter 5

1. Edwin Lefevre, *Reminiscences of a Stock Operator* (Hoboken, New Jersey: John Wiley & Sons, 2006; Originally published: New York: George H. Doran and Company, 1923)
2. Newton's First Law of Motion: https://en.wikipedia.org/wiki/Newton%27s_laws_of_motion
3. Loss Aversion: http://blog.usabilla.com/how-loss-aversion-and-risk-influence-decision-making/
4. Loss Aversion: http://wsb.wharton.upenn.edu/documents/research/IsTigerWoodsLossAverse.pdf
5. Anchoring: http://www.investopedia.com/terms/a/anchoring.asp
6. Breakeven strategy: http://www.investopedia.com/articles/02/022002.asp

Chapter 6

1. Atul Gawande, *The Check List Manifesto* (New York: Metropolitan Books, 2009)
2. Donald Rumsfeld, *Known and Unknown – A Memoir* (New York: Sentinel, a member of the Penguin Group, 2011)

Chapter 7

1) http://www.nbcnews.com/nightly-news
2. Manufactured housing shipments; http://www.census.gov/econ/currentdata/dbsearch?program=MHS&startYear=1980&endYear=1984&categories=T&dataType=SH&geoLevel=US¬Adjusted=1&submit=GET+DATA
3. Guy Fraser-Sampson, *The Pillars of Finance* (New York: Palgrave Macmillian, 2014)
4. Goldfields Ltd: http://www.bloomberg.com/apps/news?pid=newsarchive&sid=aicTmR_A56kI&refer=home
5. Goldfields Ltd: http://nypost.com/2007/04/17/the-mystery-man-responds-to-the-post/
6. Goldfields Ltd: https://en.wikipedia.org/wiki/Dan_Pastorini

7. Goldfields Ltd: https://www.goldfields.co.za/med_news_article.php?articleID=55
8. https://en.wikipedia.org/wiki/List_of_best_Major_League_Baseball_season_won-loss_records
9. http://www.dailypress.com/dp-top100-grahamsep24-story
10. Tali Sharot, The Optimism Bias (New York: Vintage Books, A division of Random House, Inc., 2011)

Chapter 8

1. Savviness definition: http://dictionary.reference.com/browse/savviness

Chapter 9

1. Edwin Lefevre, *Reminiscences of a Stock Operator* (Hoboken, New Jersey: John Wiley & Sons, 2006; Originally published: New York: George H. Doran and Company, 1923)
2. Fear of regret: http://www.investopedia.com/terms/r/regrettheory.asp
3. Greg McKeown, *Essentialism* (New York, Crown Business, 2014)
4. http://www.inc.com/christina-desmarais/30-ceos-reveal-the-daily-habits-responsible-for-their-success.html

Index

D

E

F

G

H

I

J

K

L

M

N

O

P

Q

R